THE BRIGHTON & HOVE PHOTOGRAPHIC COLLECTION

VOLUME 1

INTRODUCTION

For many years, people have contacted QueenSpark Books about photographs; they've wanted us to find them, archive them, identify them, or publish them – and in most cases we've had to say 'no', as we've had neither the physical space, nor the expertise, to do so.

However, two years ago we decided that we had to do something, and sought the support of the Heritage Lottery Fund to enable us to create a 'people's photographic history' of Brighton & Hove – one that everybody can see, and to which everybody can contribute.

For the last twelve months we have been collecting photographs – and the comments which appear throughout this book – at community events, media appeals, and via our website. The hundreds of photographs already collected at **www.photosbrightonandhove.org.uk** form a fascinating archive of our city's history. However, at QueenSpark we are very aware that 'history starts today'; a current photograph – maybe one that doesn't appear that interesting on the surface – acquires resonance through the years. This is why The Brighton & Hove Photographic Collection includes contemporary as well as historic photographs; so if you've taken an interesting photograph today, we'd love to see it – and we're sure that others would too.

We are also very grateful to the amateur and professional photographers and collectors who have submitted photographs in person or online, and the wonderful local people – listed inside the back cover – who have financially supported this book.

This book is 'Volume 1' – and we would very much like your help to produce further volumes. Please get snapping or dig out your old photographs, and send them to us, and maybe you can feature in the next book!

QueenSpark Books

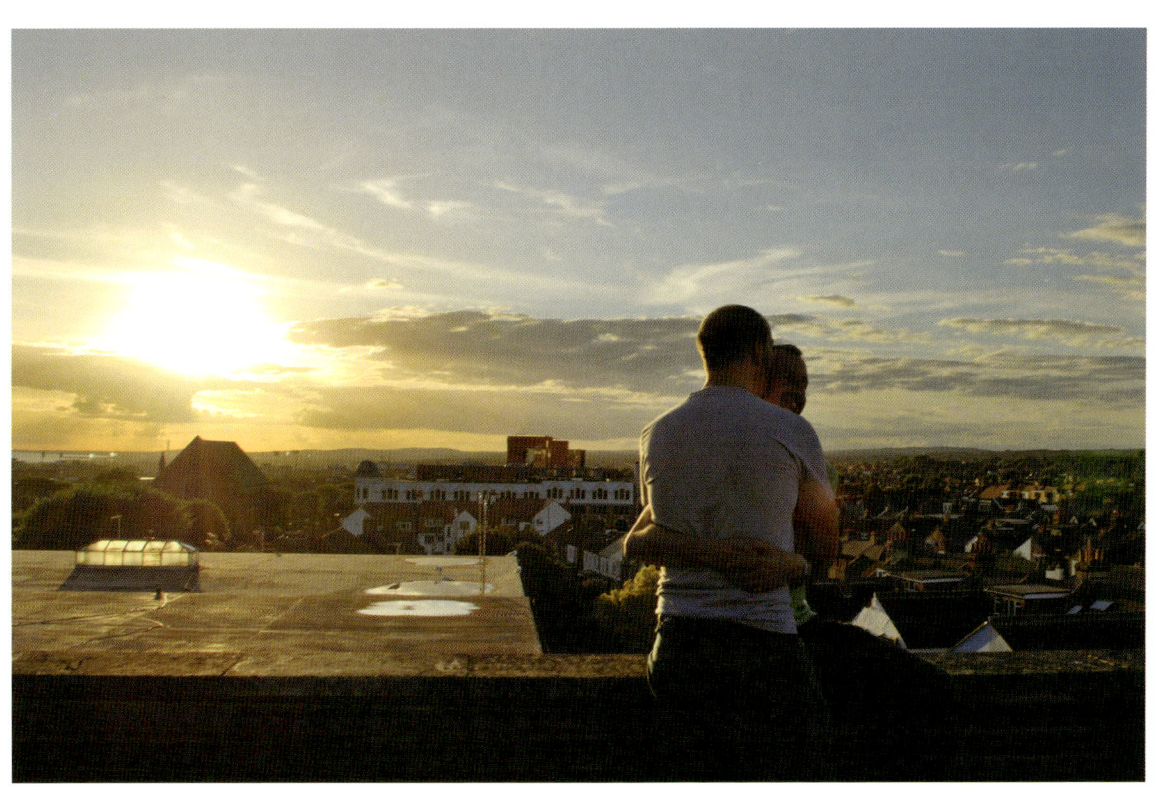

THE EMBRACE

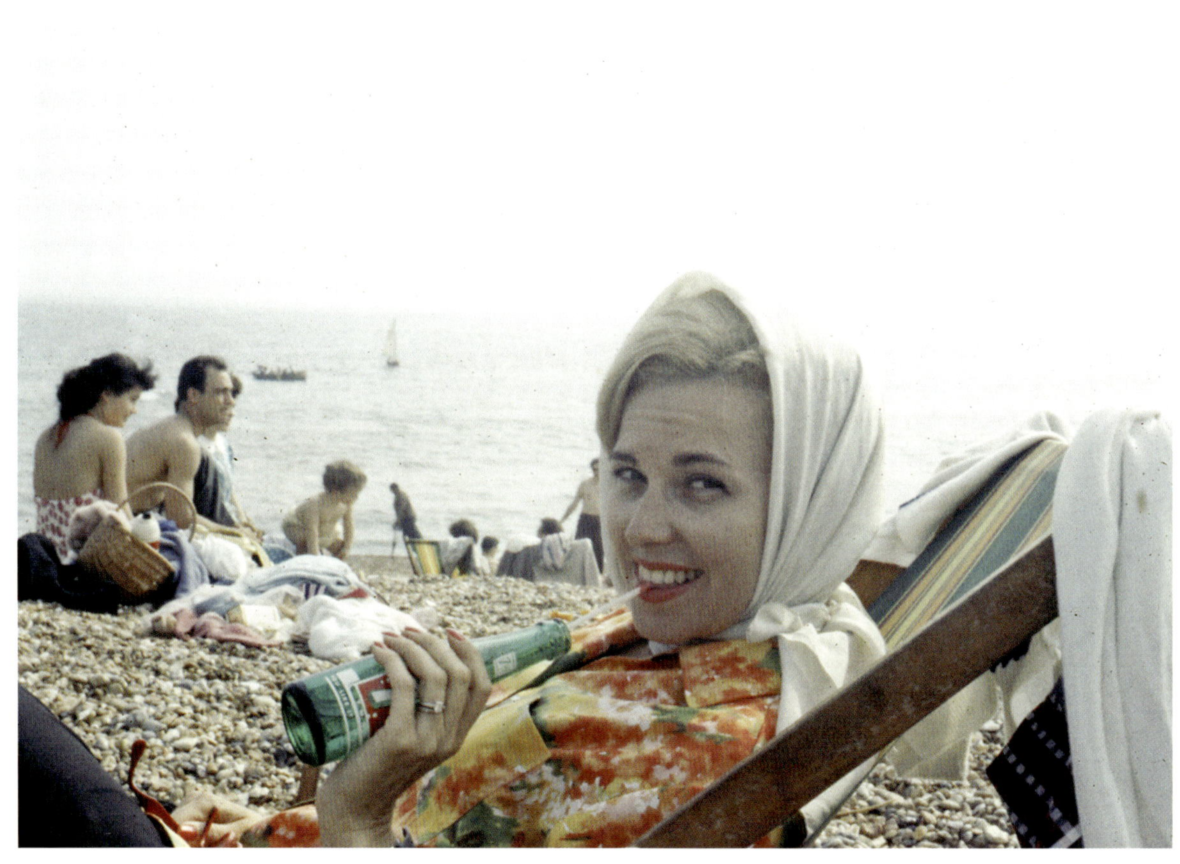

ON THE BEACH AT BRIGHTON, 1960

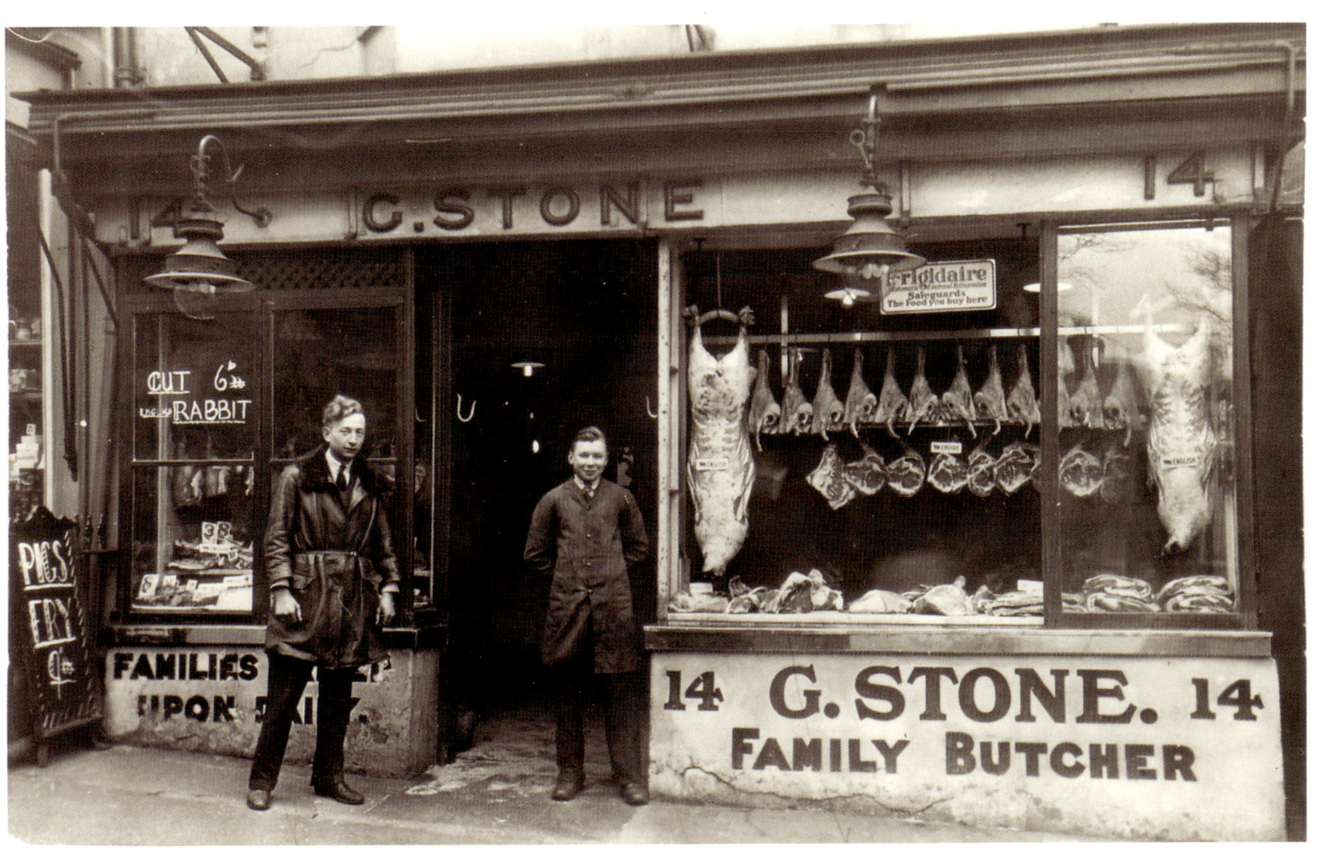

STONES THE BUTCHERS

"This was in Elm Grove and I lived nearby in Arnold Street when I was seven. I remember Mr Stone himself." – Dawn

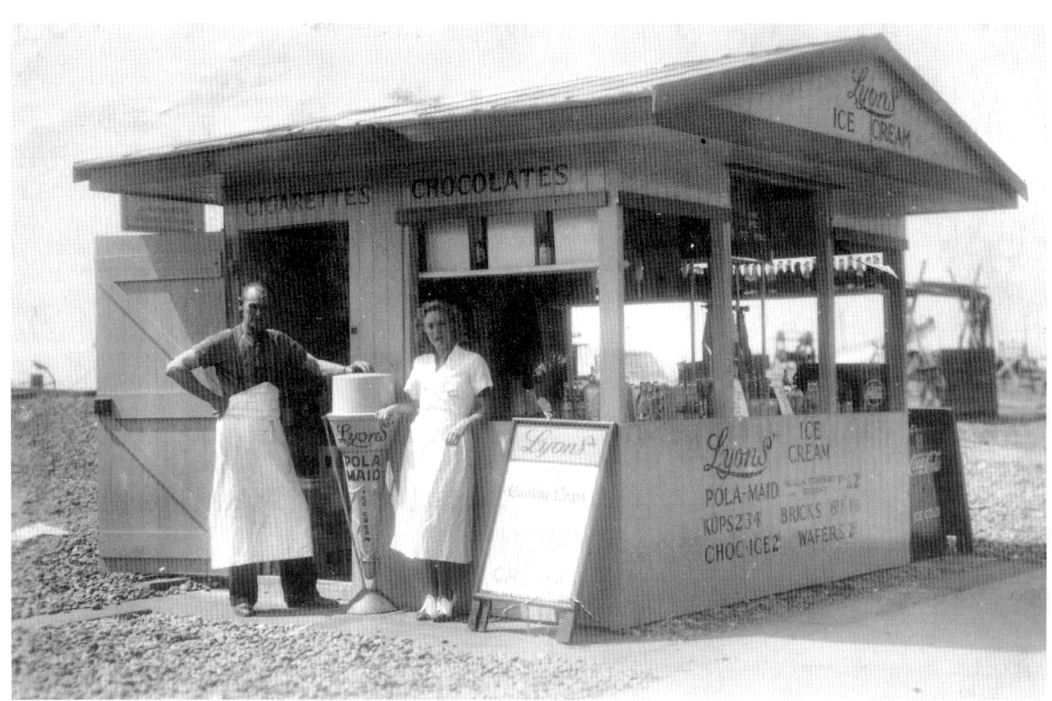

BEACH CAFE, C.1930

"I'm not old enough to remember this cafe but I do remember the beach trays you could buy at seaside cafes. You would get a proper tray with a china pot of tea and a jug of hot water and could take it down to where you were sitting on the beach. No deposit was needed, they trusted you to bring it all back!" – Kathy

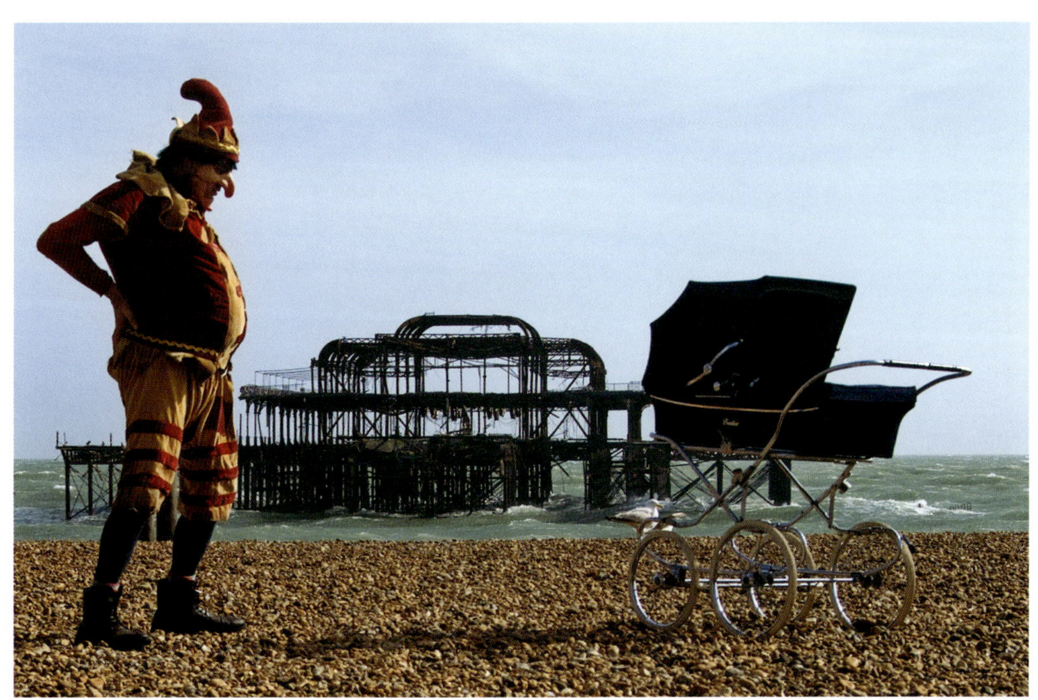

MR PUNCH

©JJ Waller

"There used to be a real character in the 80's doing Punch and Judy shows, Mike Stone. He worked down the seafront and also did shows at pubs where it was a darker, sometimes very blue show. My friends and I used to go out especially to see him." – Debbie

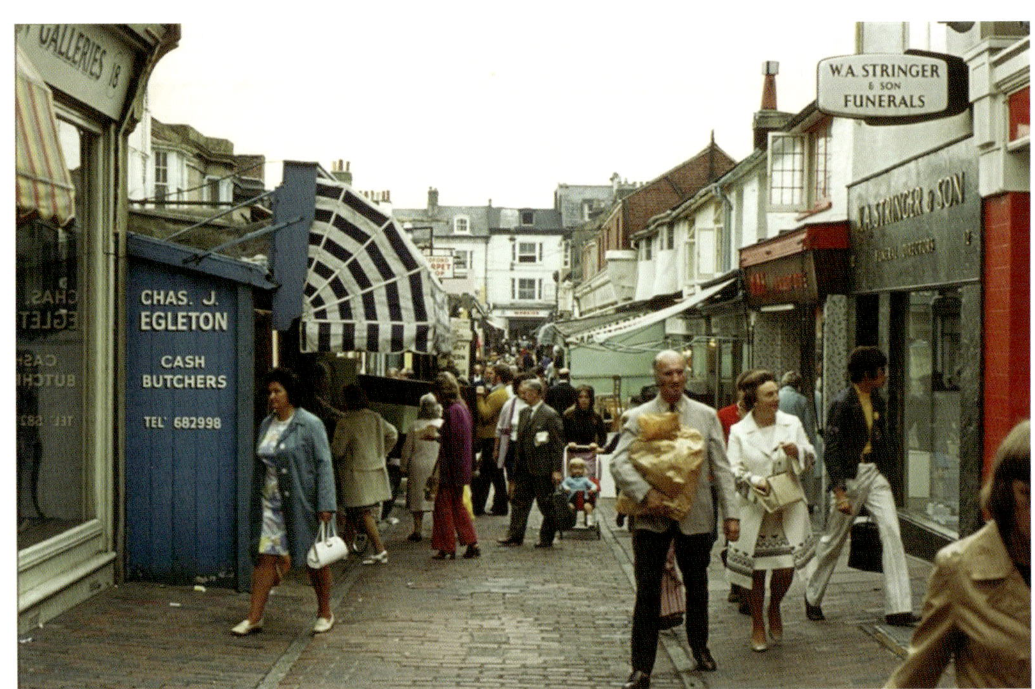

KENSINGTON GARDENS, 1972

©Reinard Clasen

"I remember there being a wallpaper shop along here. Also Blundells (I think it was called) a big Department store. It's now a giant "flea market". My Mum really embarrassed me in there when I was 12 and she shouted to the shop worker "Do you do the junior training bras?" I think that was the last time I ever went there. They also had a van that came round the estates crammed with stuff you could choose and pay off a bit a week." – Dawn

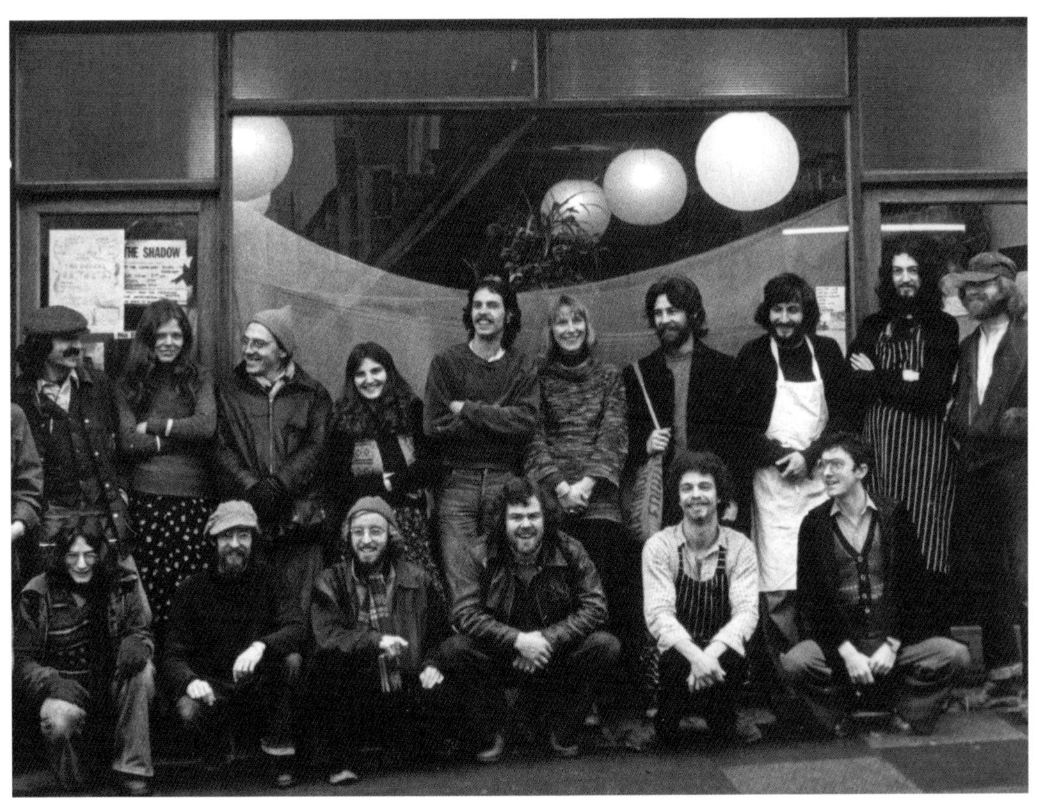

WORKERS AT INFINITY FOODS, C.1976

"I know so many people in this picture. Where has the last 30 years gone? So much more hair back then!" – Richard

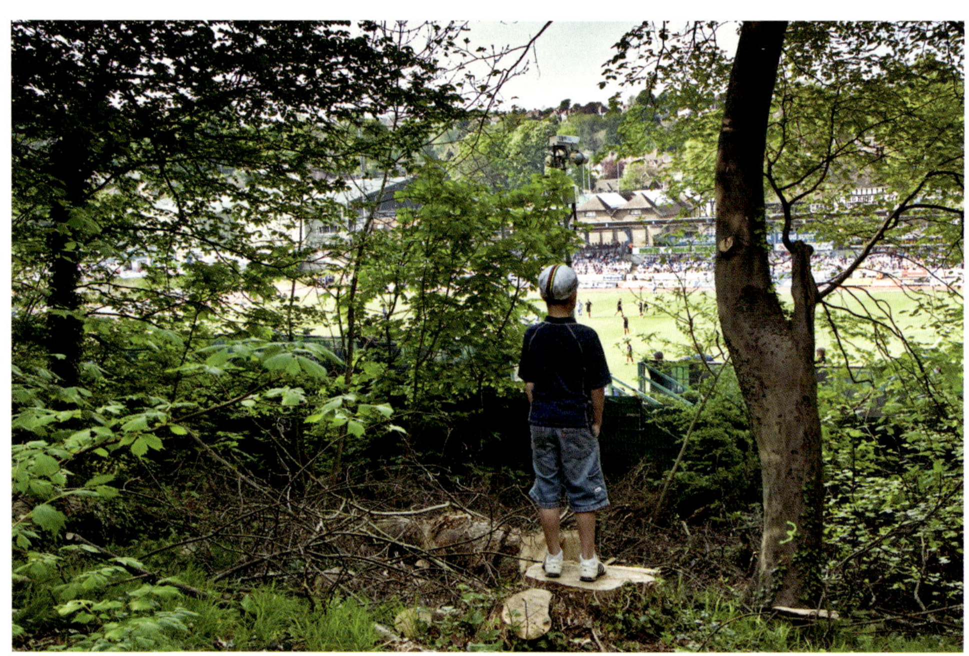

STADIUM OF TREES - LAST GAME AT WITHDEAN, APRIL 2011

"At every home game, the stewards embarked on a fruitless mission to clear the Nature Reserve and flush out ticketless fans." – Roz

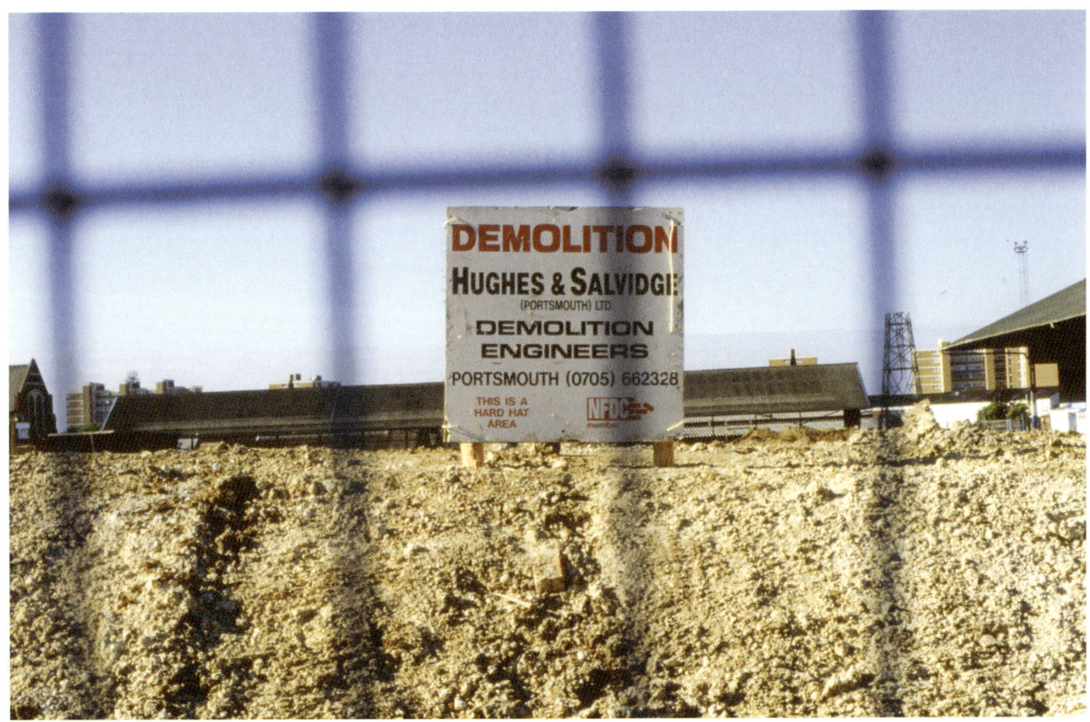

GOODBYE GOLDSTONE, 1997

©JJ Waller

"I went to a Half Man Half Biscuit gig in aid of the Seagulls when the Goldstone Ground was closing down. There were expressions of support from football fans worldwide and loads came to support the team from all over the country." – Nicola

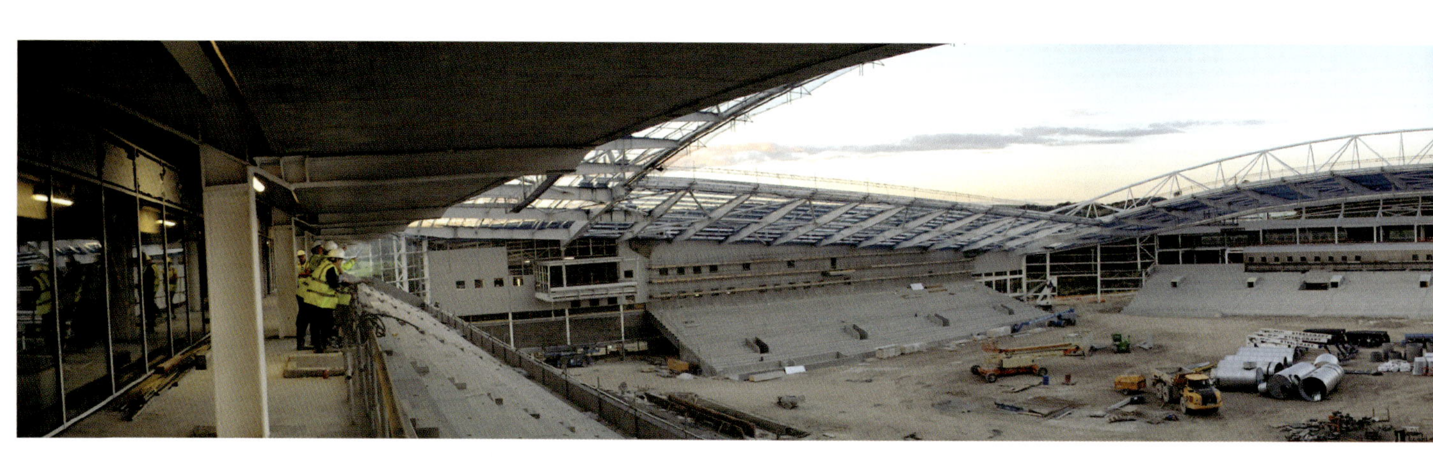

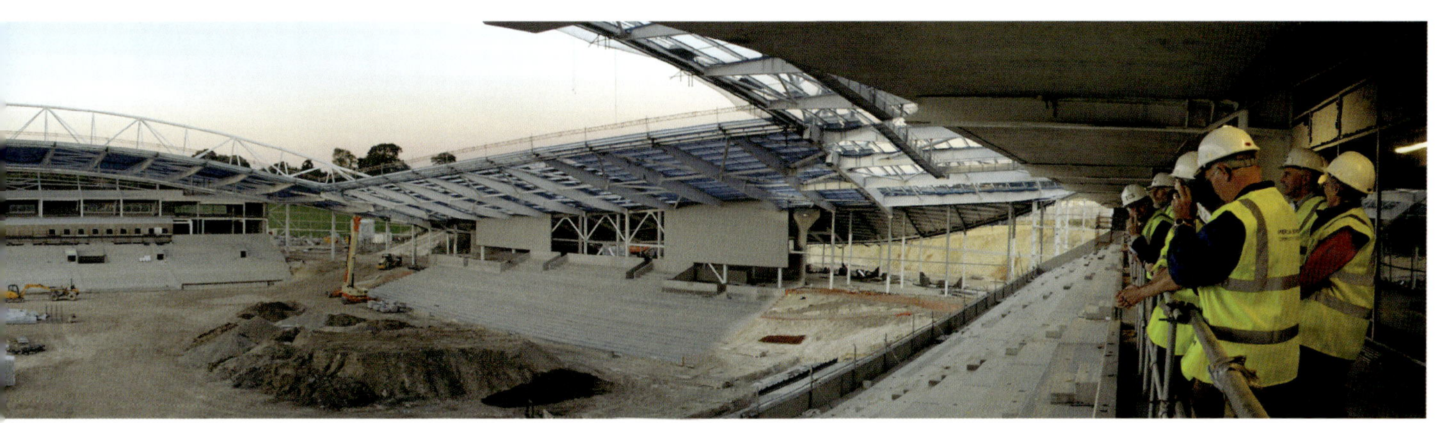

AMEX STADIUM ON THE WAY TO COMPLETION, 2010

"An exciting part of Brighton's future. One day this picture will be part of the history of the stadium." – Zoe

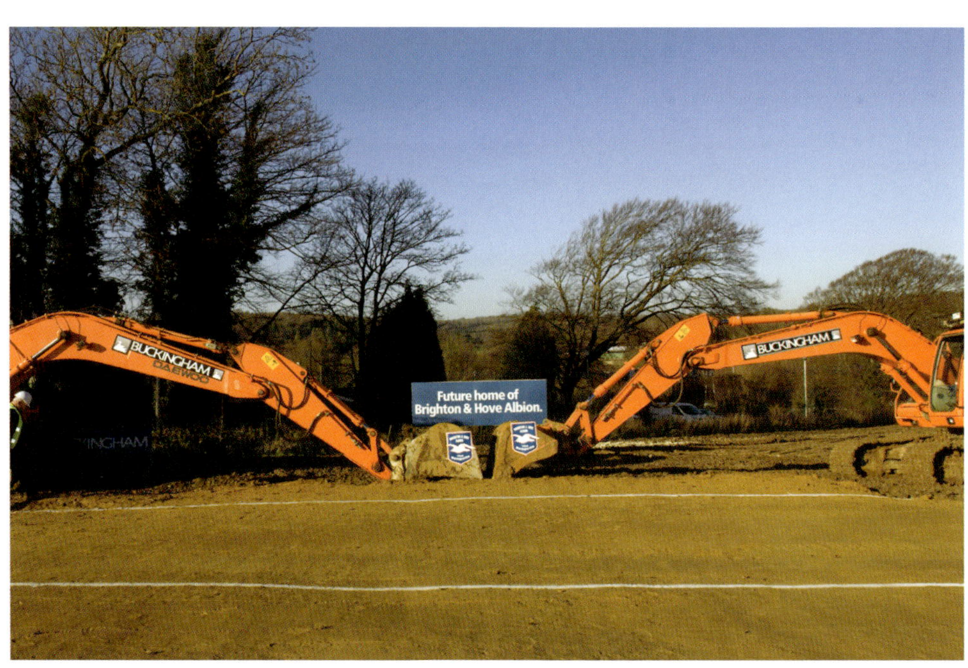

CONSTRUCTION OFFICIALLY STARTS AT THE AMEX STADIUM, 2007

"I was at the last game at the Goldstone in 1997 and I still can't bring myself to drive past the place but the journey past Falmer is now a joy." – Ed

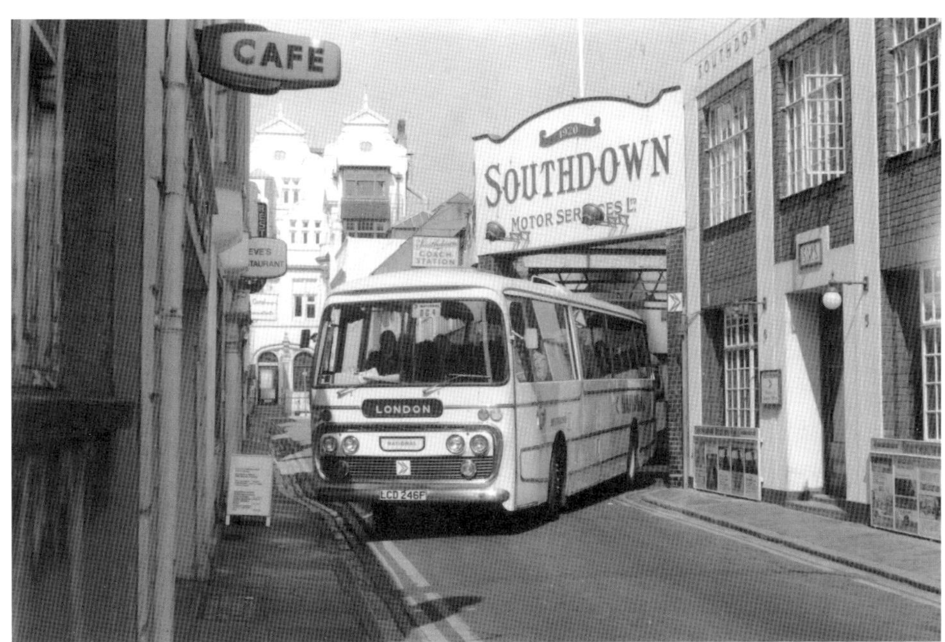

LONDON BOUND COACH LEAVES STEINE STREET COACH STATION, 1971

"Up in the corner there was a big old restaurant called Charlies. All the luxury coaches used to come into the coach station. How they did it I don't know because it was so narrow. – Maurice

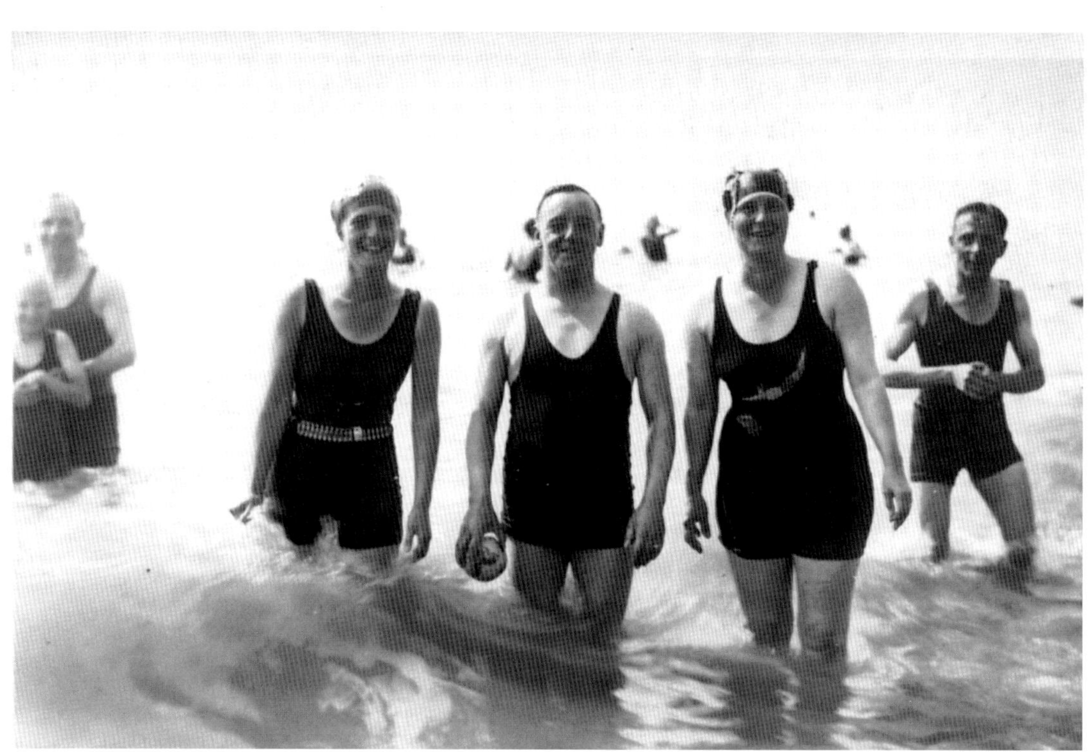

BATHERS AT HOVE BEACH, 1931

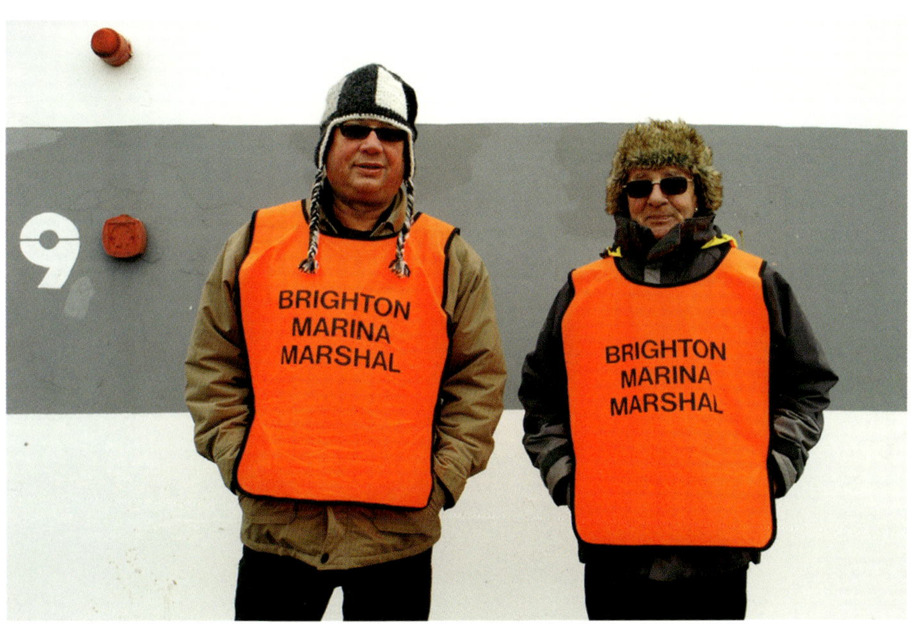

BRIGHTON MARINA MARKET MARSHALS

©David Sutherland

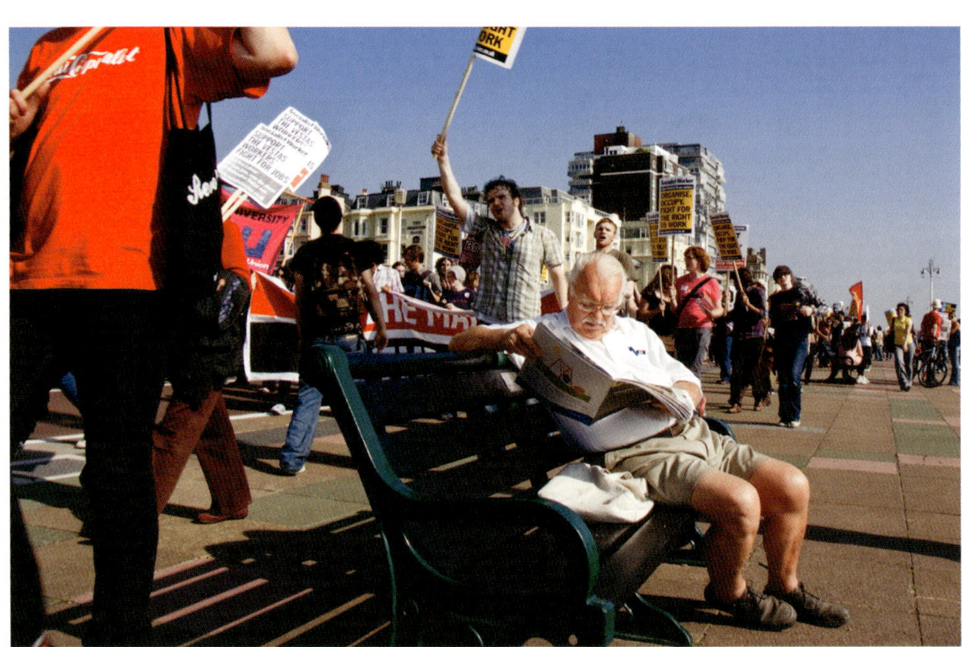

BREAKING NEWS

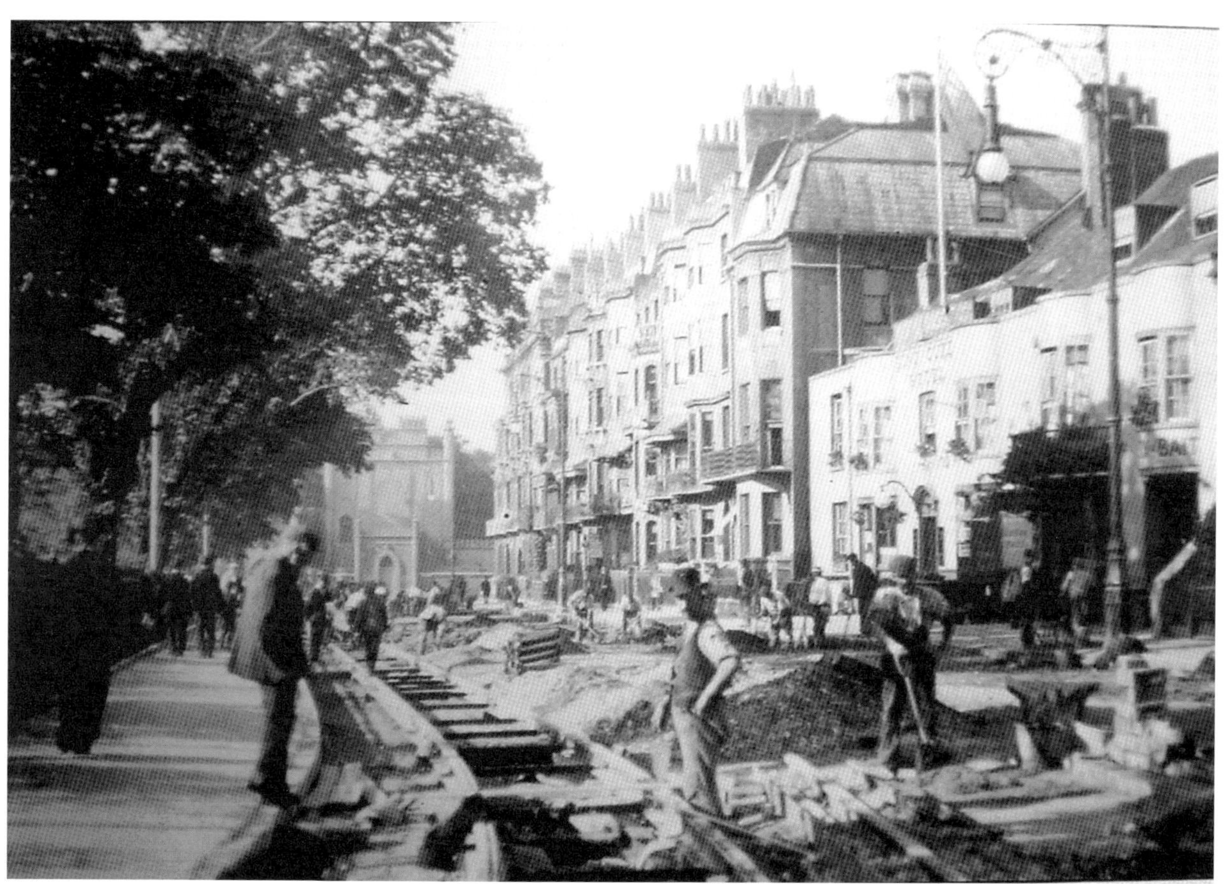

LAYING TRAMLINES, VICTORIA GARDENS, 1901

"My Dad remembers the Corporation covering the trams with a wire screen during the General Strike in 1926. This was so that the windows couldn't be smashed by strikers." – Linda

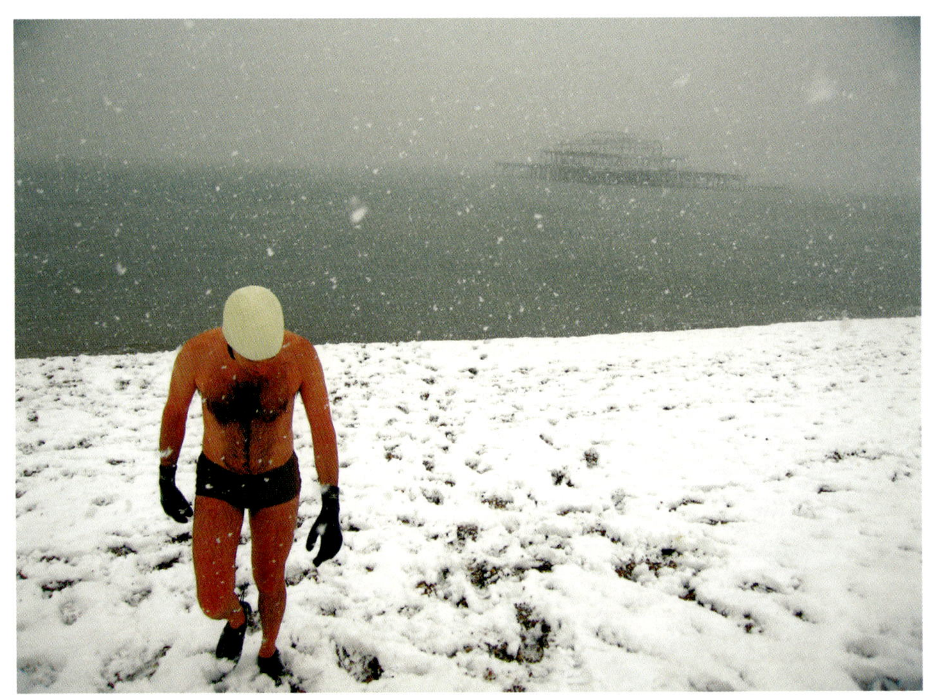

SNOWY BATHER

©Yvonne Luna

"This is me! It was a freaky, snowstormy day in April so I had to go down to the sea and swim in it!" – Nick

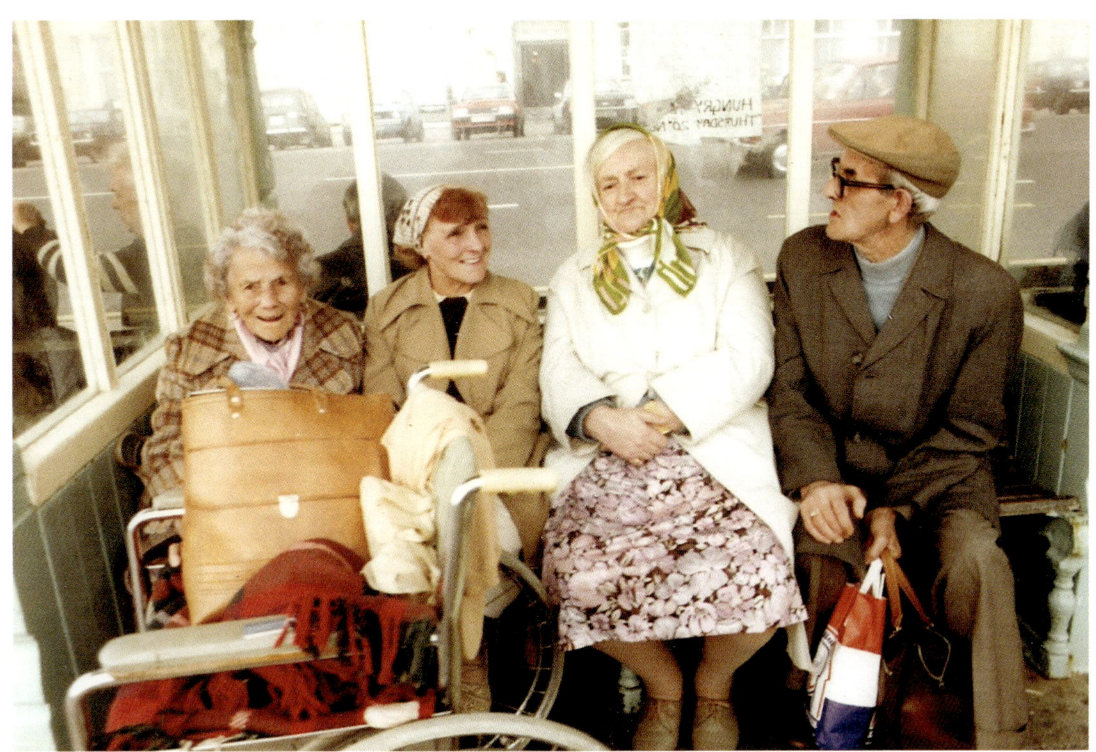

SEASIDE SHELTER IN THE 1980S

"The colours and the people in the picture remind me of a typical seaside holiday in Brighton when it was a traditional and rather run down resort" – Deidre

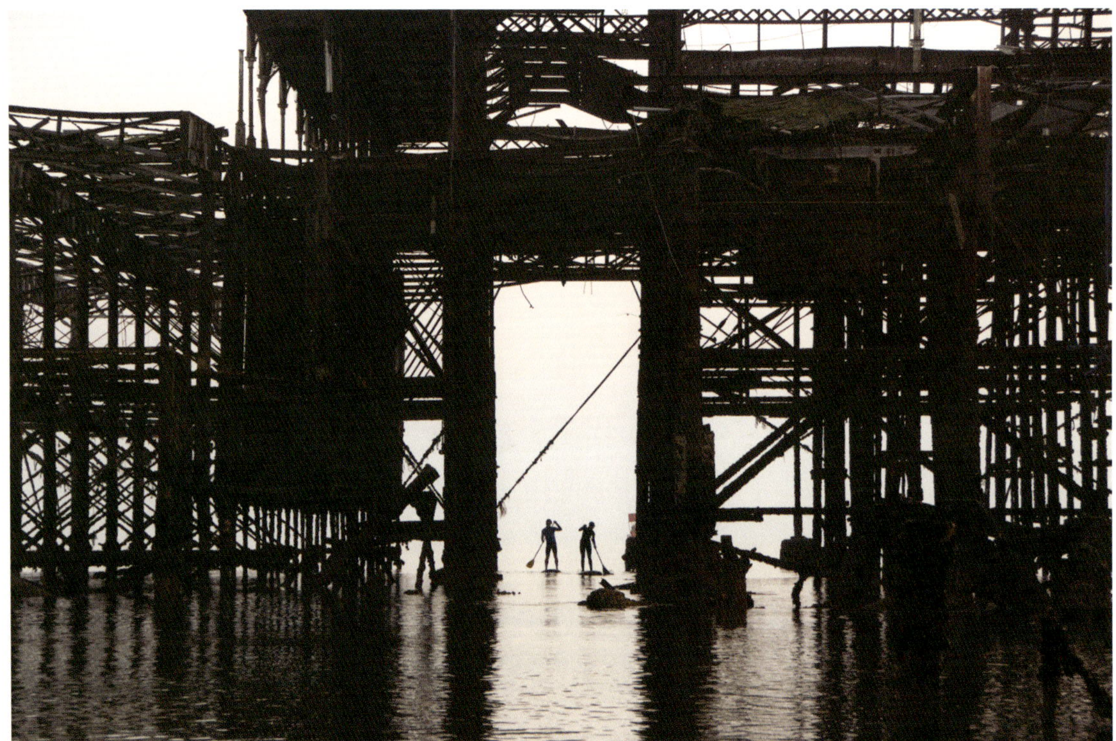

UNDER THE WEST PIER

"This is dramatic but I fear it is an accident waiting to happen and rumour has it that there is a million pounds worth of listed scrap on the seabed." – Catherine

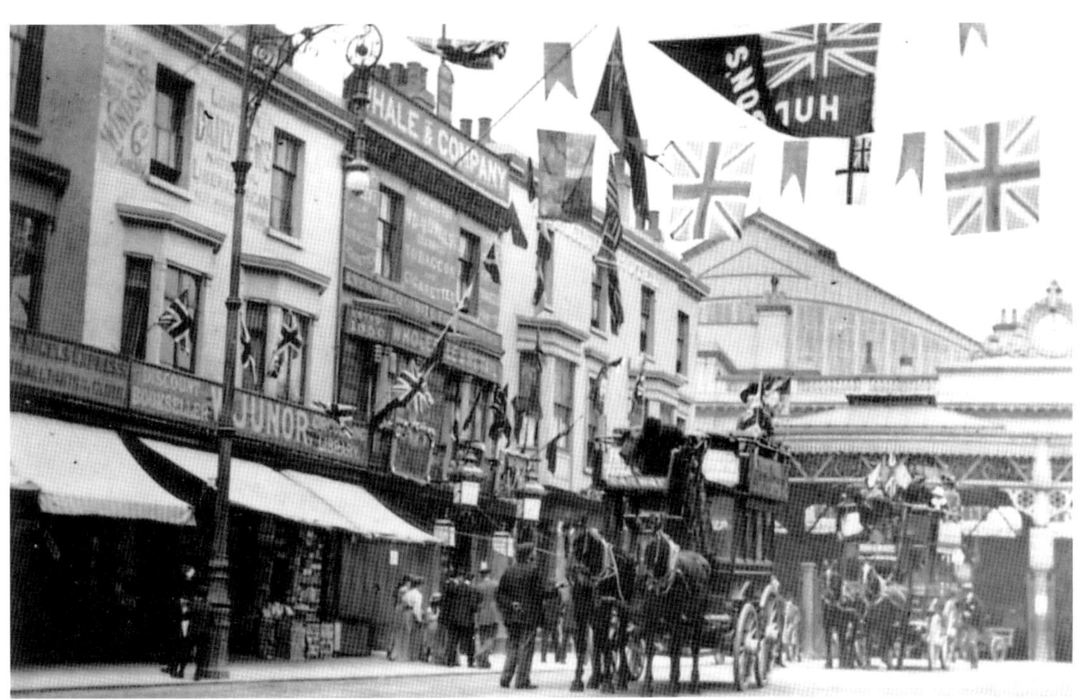

BRIGHTON STATION & QUEEN'S ROAD WITH BUNTING, C.1887

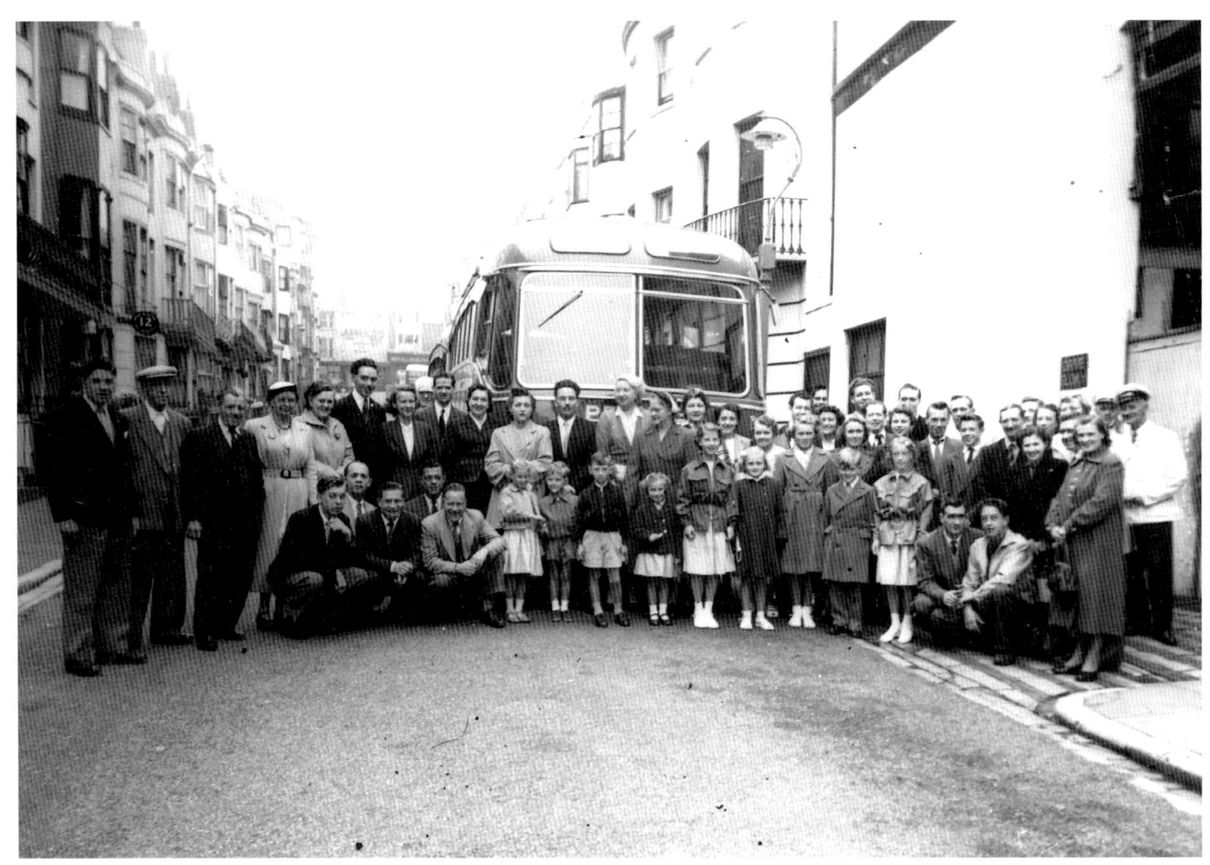

BRIGHTON SHEET METAL WORKERS ANNUAL OUTING – MANCHESTER STREET, 1947

"This reminds me of when I worked for Dentsply in Coombe Road. We had all sorts of outings. They would lay on six coaches, unbelievable and really nice." – George

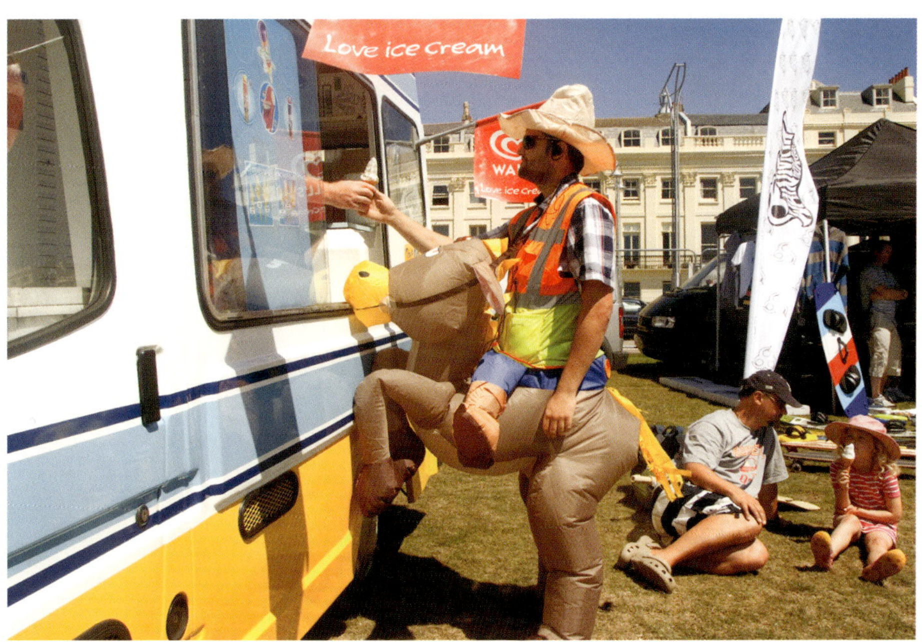

ICE-CREAM COWBOY

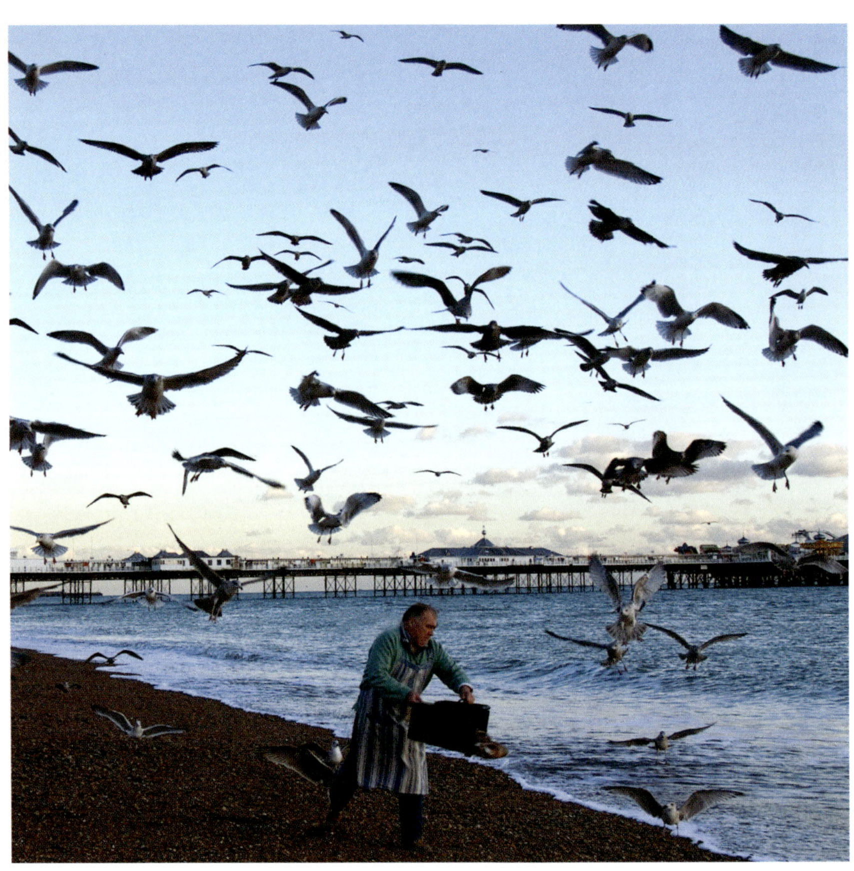

FISH, GULLS, PIER

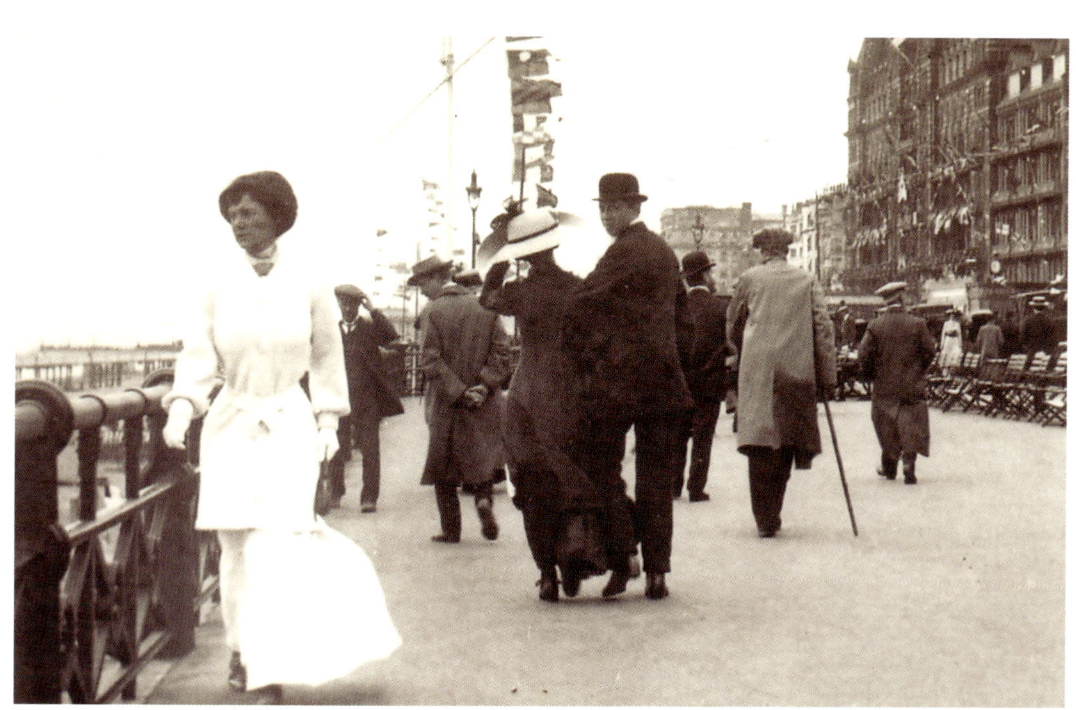

WINDY SEAFRONT, C.1890

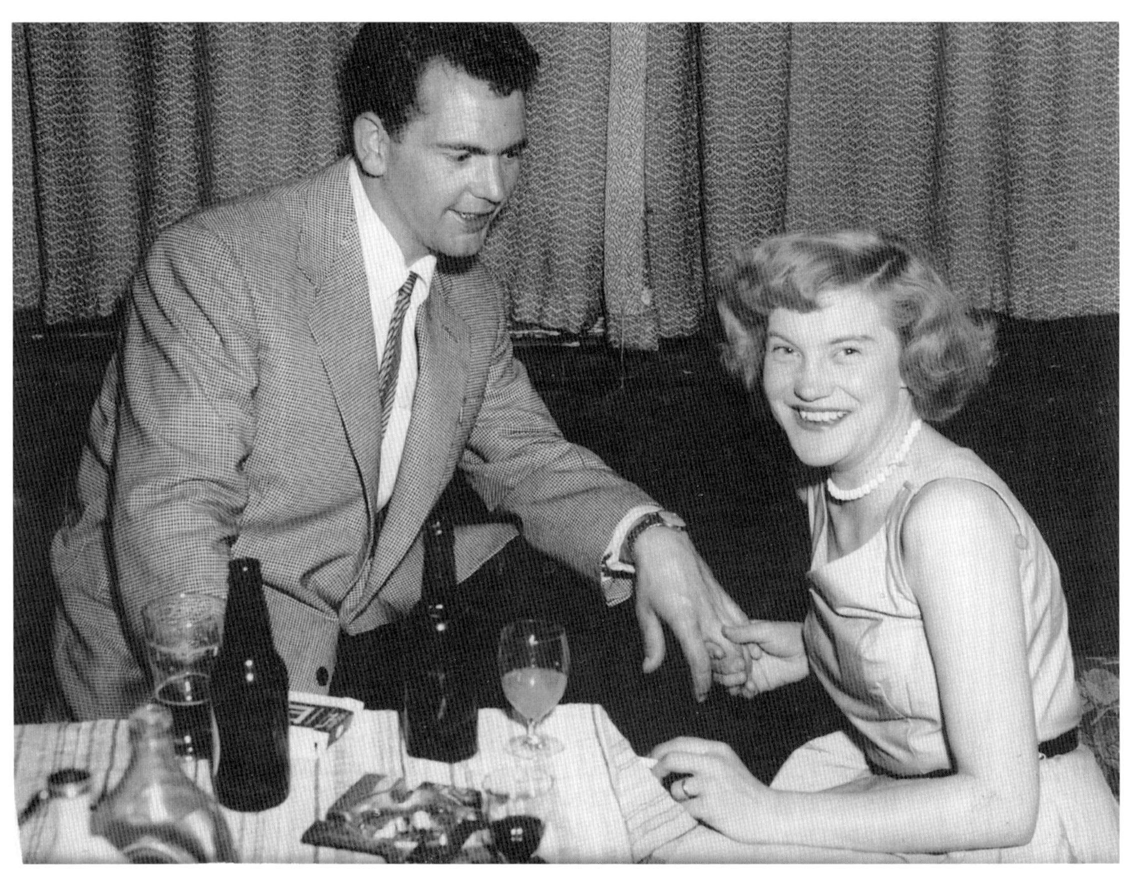

BRIGHTON HONEYMOON AT HARRISON'S HOTEL, 1953

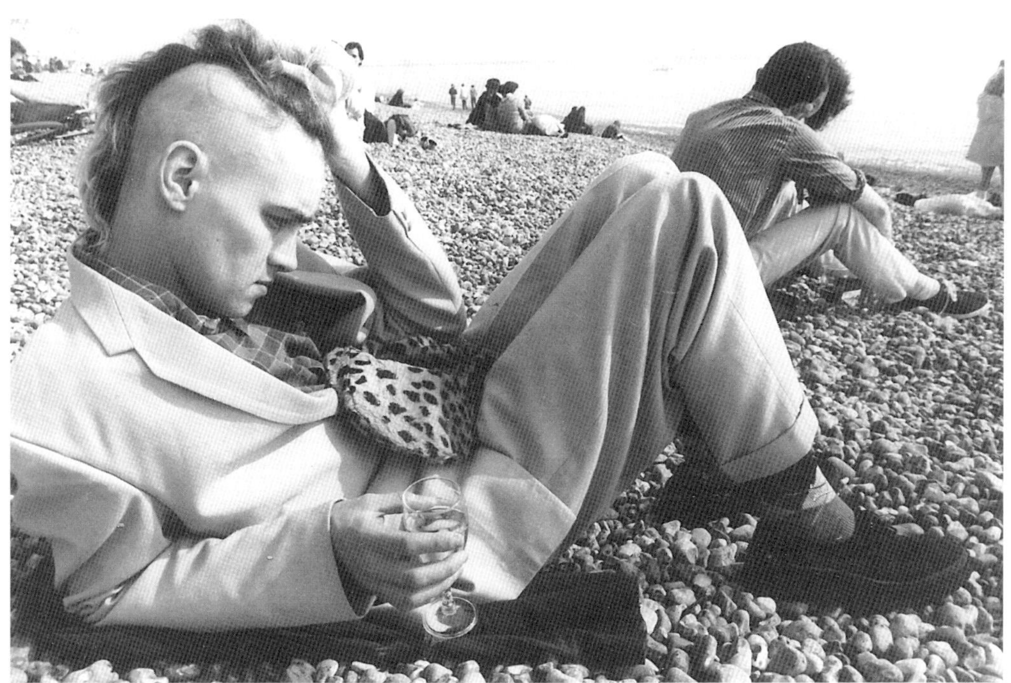

JONATHAN ON THE BEACH, 19 MARCH 1982

"Although this is '82 it reminds me of 1977 when I was on holiday in Brighton and Elvis had just died. I remember walking along the seafront, which was littered with punks and Teddy boys alike, most of whom were crying. An image I can distinctly remember is a very drunk Teddy Boy sheltering under a fishing boat for the night, bottle in hand with just his brothel creepers peeping out." – Sarah

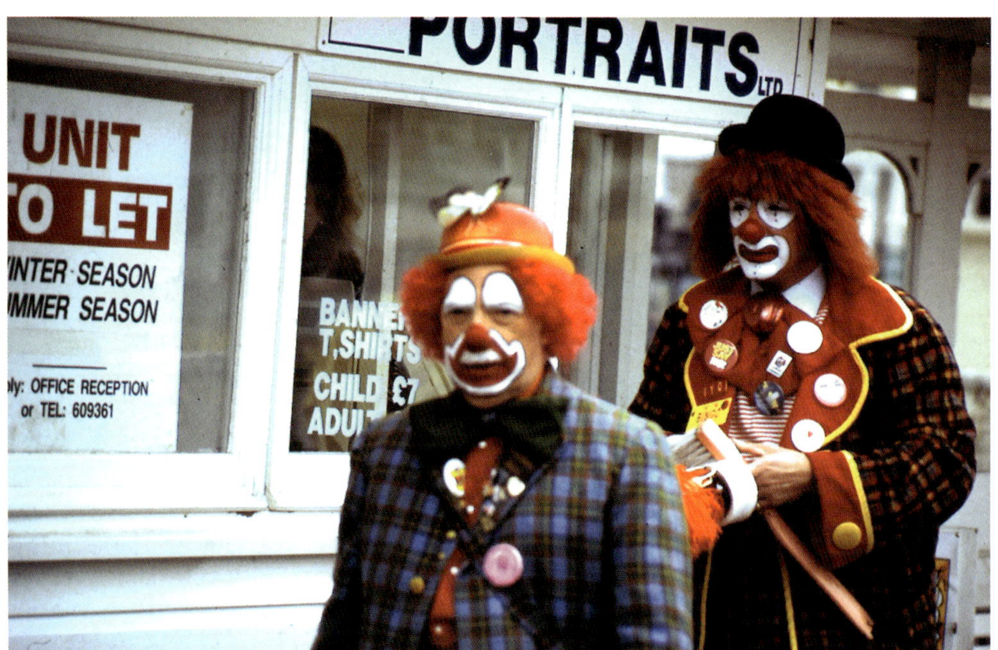

CLOWN CONVENTION, APRIL 1991

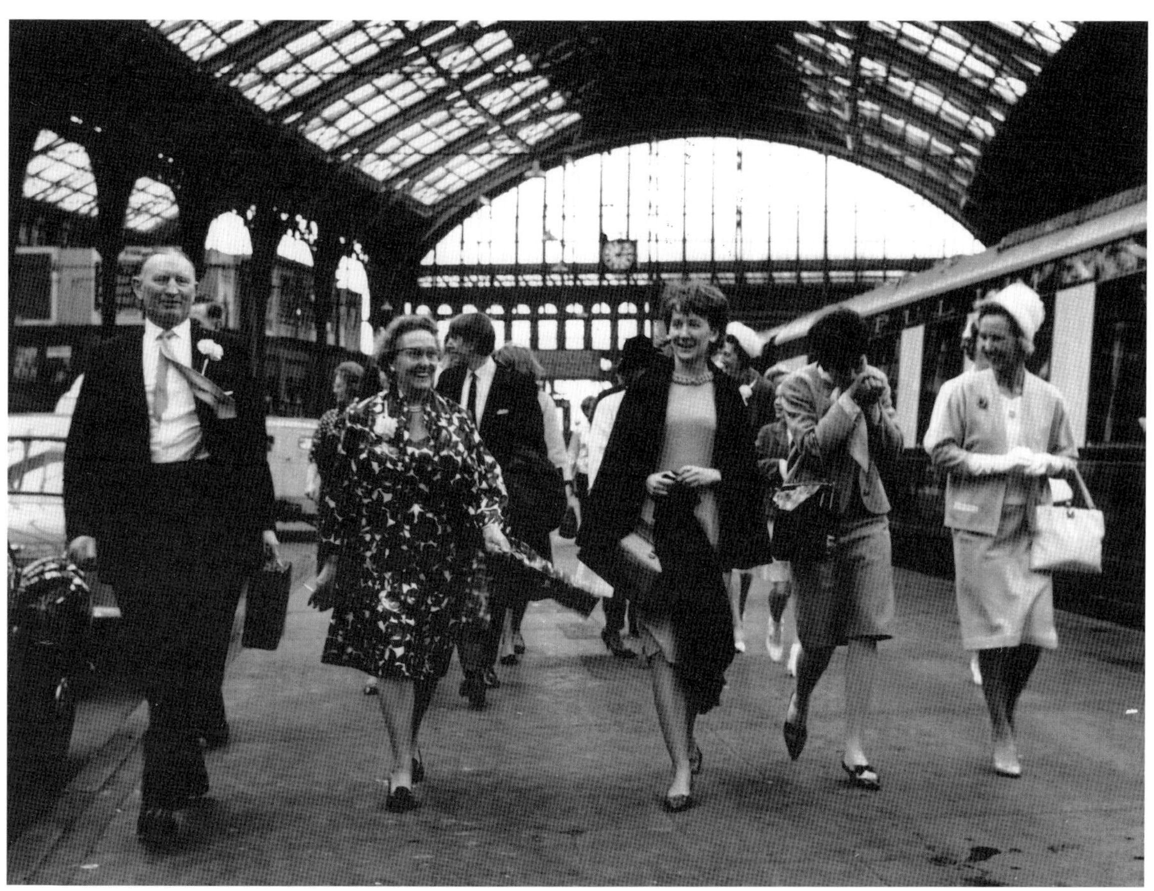

THE GOING AWAY PARTY - BRIGHTON STATION, 1963

"Lovely clothes and I like the way that the elegant lady is lighting a cigarette! – Liz

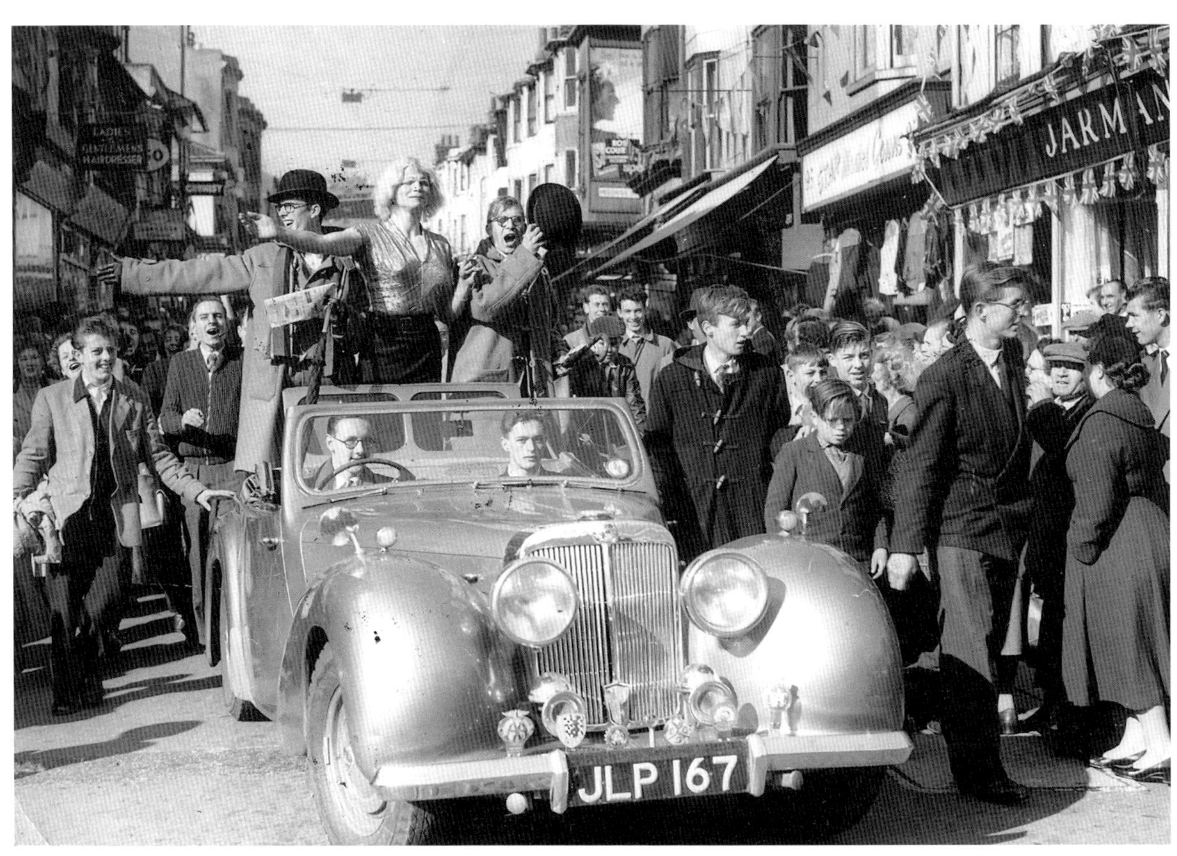

RAG WEEK IN TRAFALGAR STREET, 1955

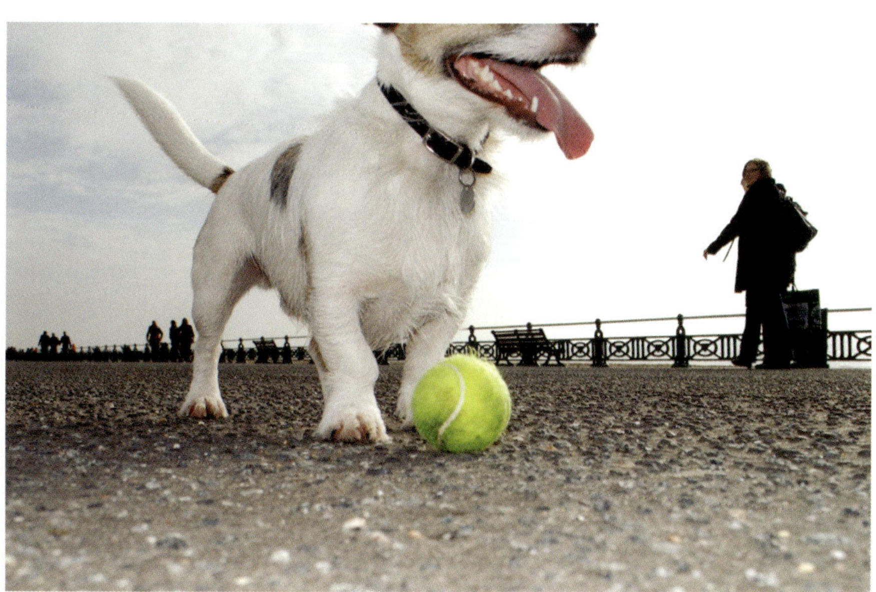

THE LITTLE DOG LAUGHED

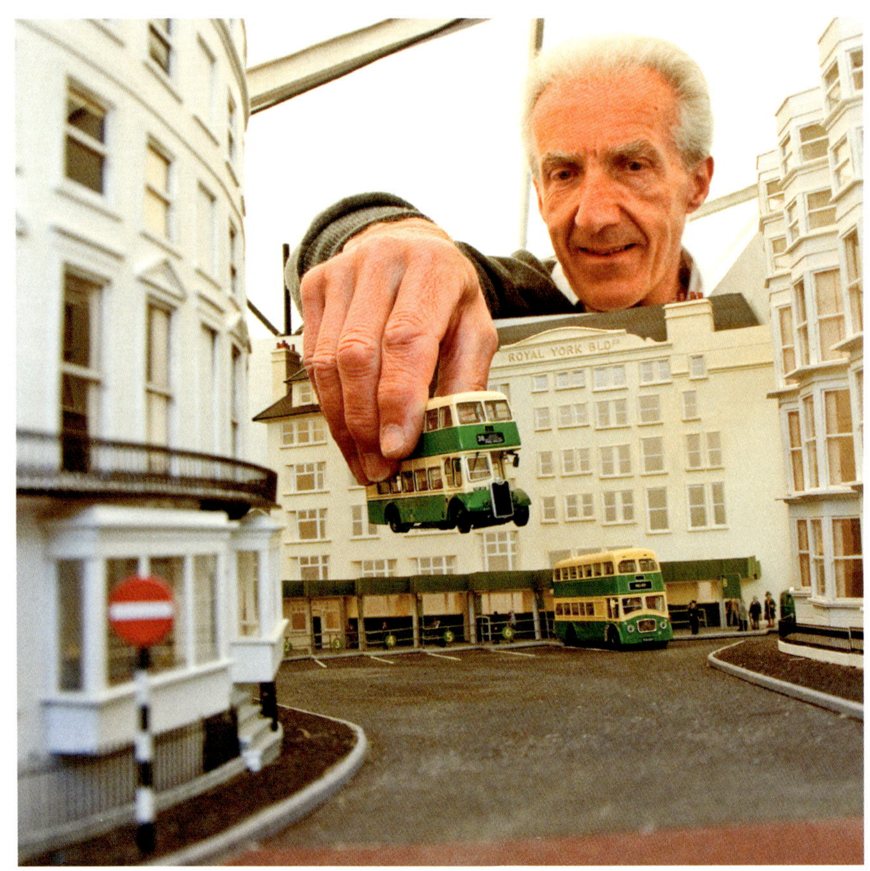

A PERSPECTIVE OF POOL VALLEY

©JJ Waller

"There's a model Southdown bus for kids to ride on in London Road now. The other day he stopped it for a minute and got a parking ticket!" – Mary

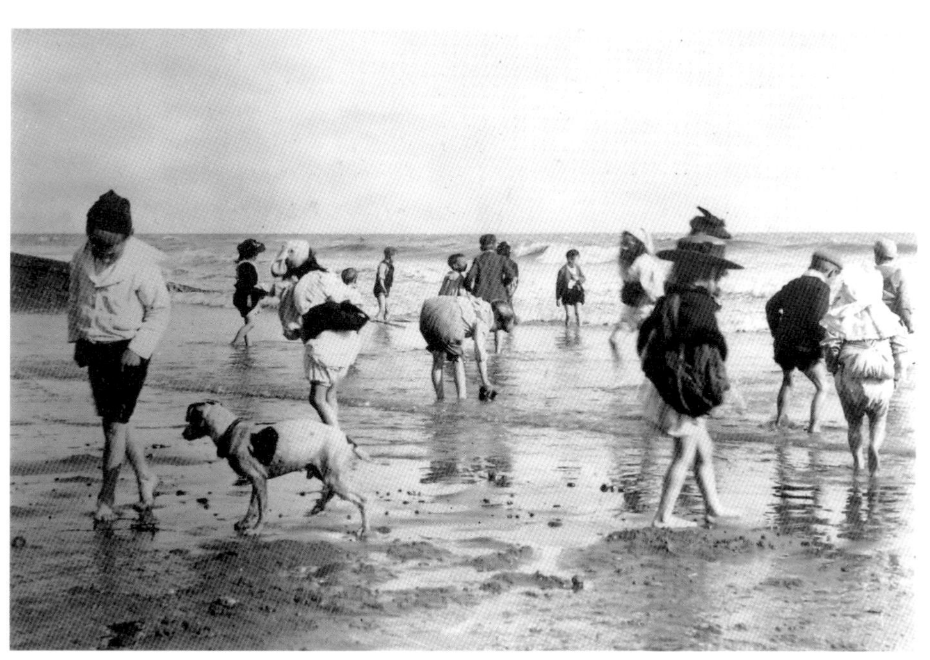

PADDLERS, C.1890

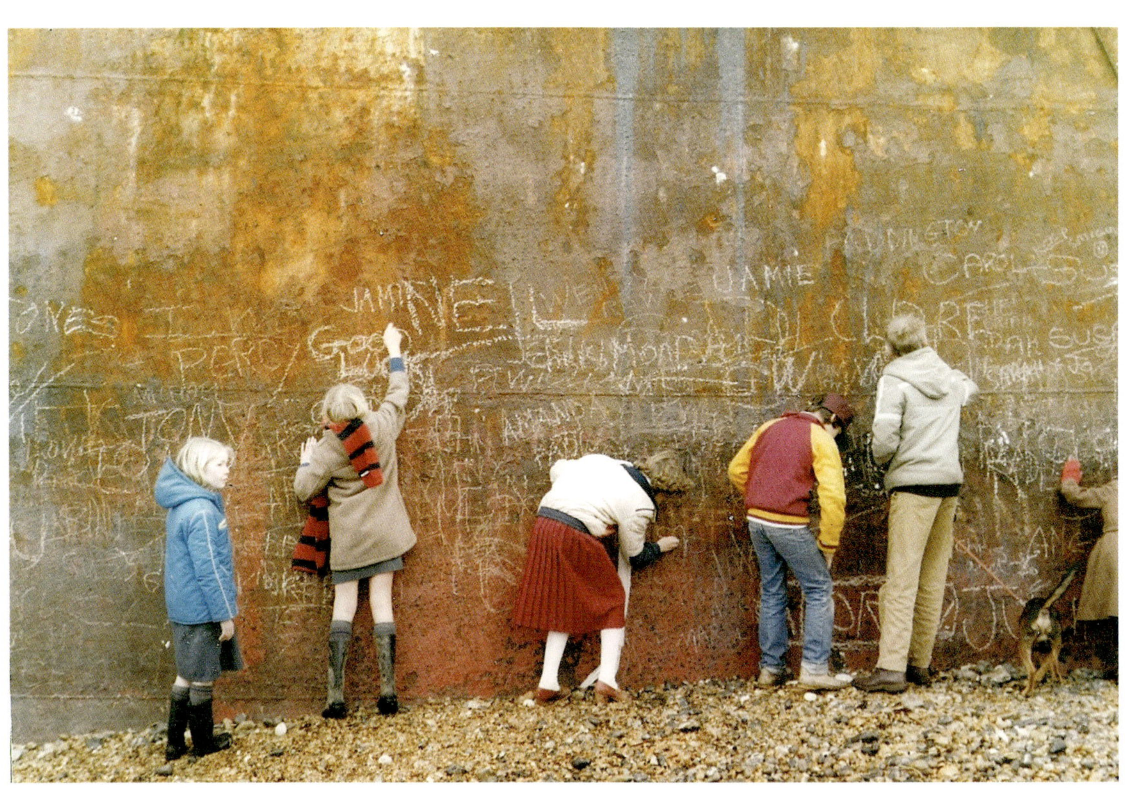

DECORATING THE ATHINA B

My Mum took us down. I must have been seven. We were looking for bits of pumice to pick up – that's what it was carrying." – Andrea

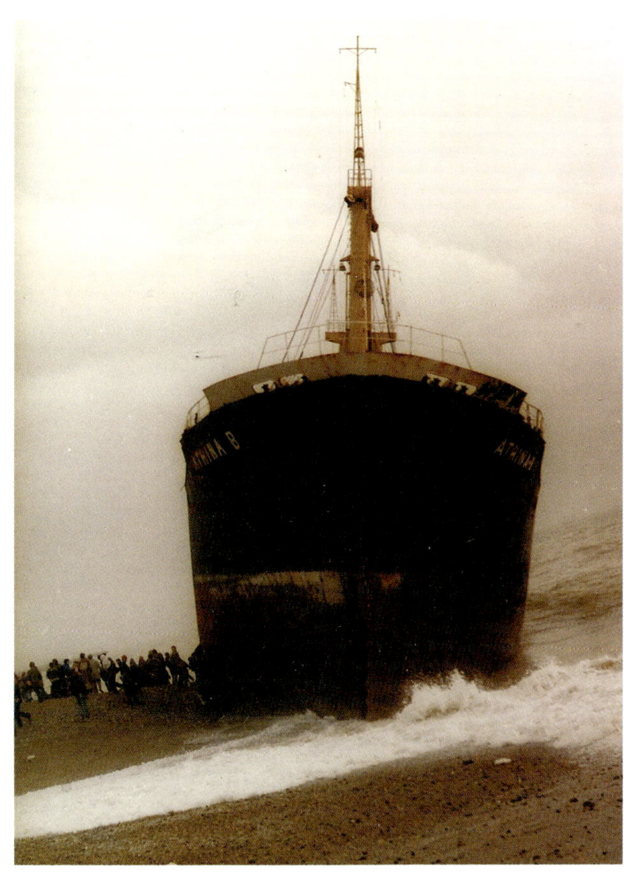

ATHINA B ON BRIGHTON BEACH, JANUARY 1980

©Peter Chrisp

"We all went down to see it go but it was so foggy nobody could see it...and they left the anchor behind!" – Bill

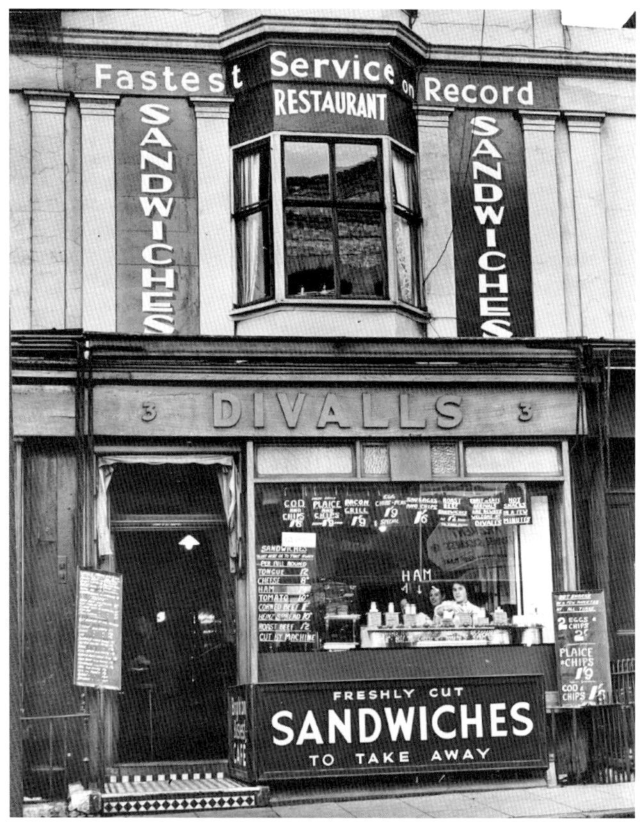

DIVALLS CAFE

"There were several Divalls Cafes. Middle Street, at the Station and Preston Circus amongst them. There was a hole in the counter top and they tied the spoon up through it so you had to stir your tea before you sat down." – Maurice

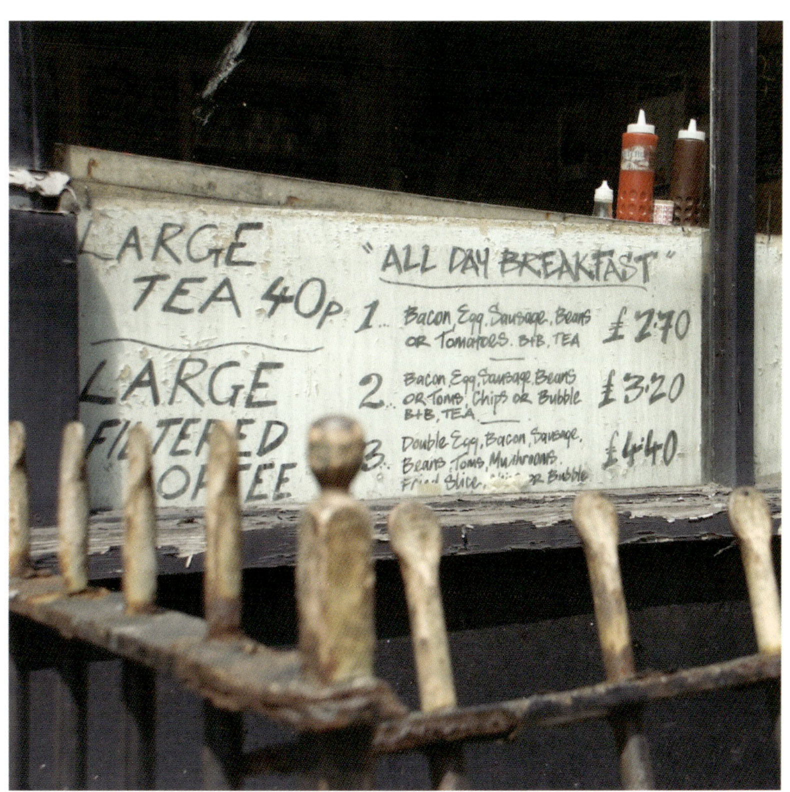

DIVALLS CAFE 2007

©JJ Waller

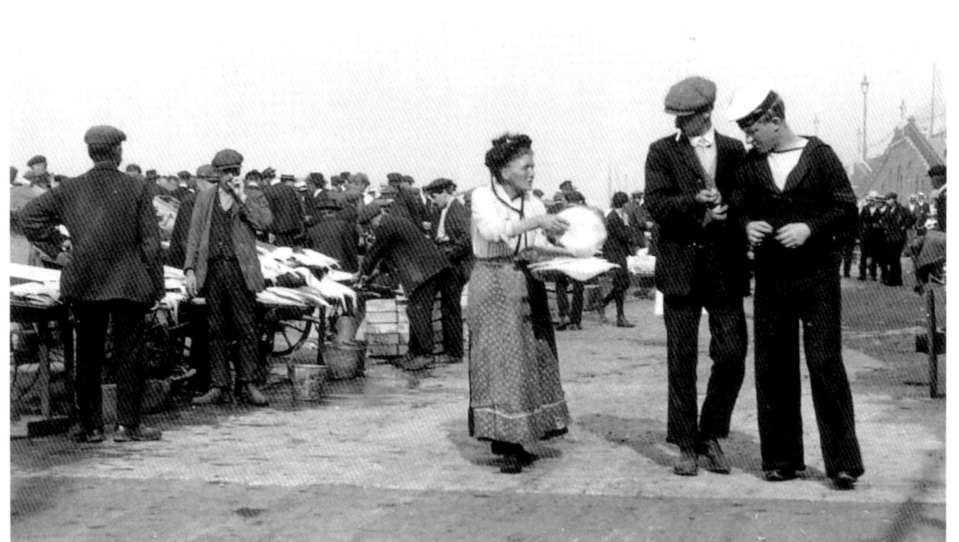

SEAFRONT WITH SAILORS AND STREET VENDOR, C.1890

"When I was young, they used to come all around the streets to sell fish, calling out 'Mackerel Alive Oh! Dozen a shilling'." – Maurice

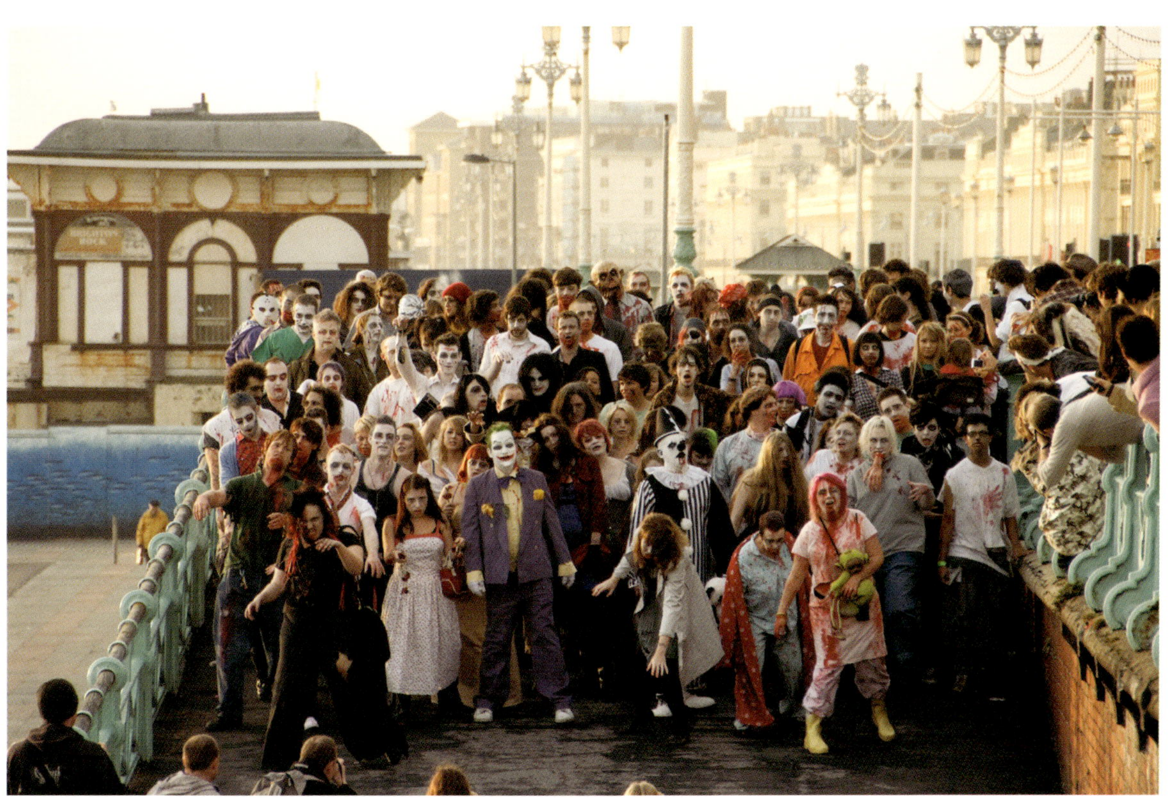

ZOMBIE DAWN

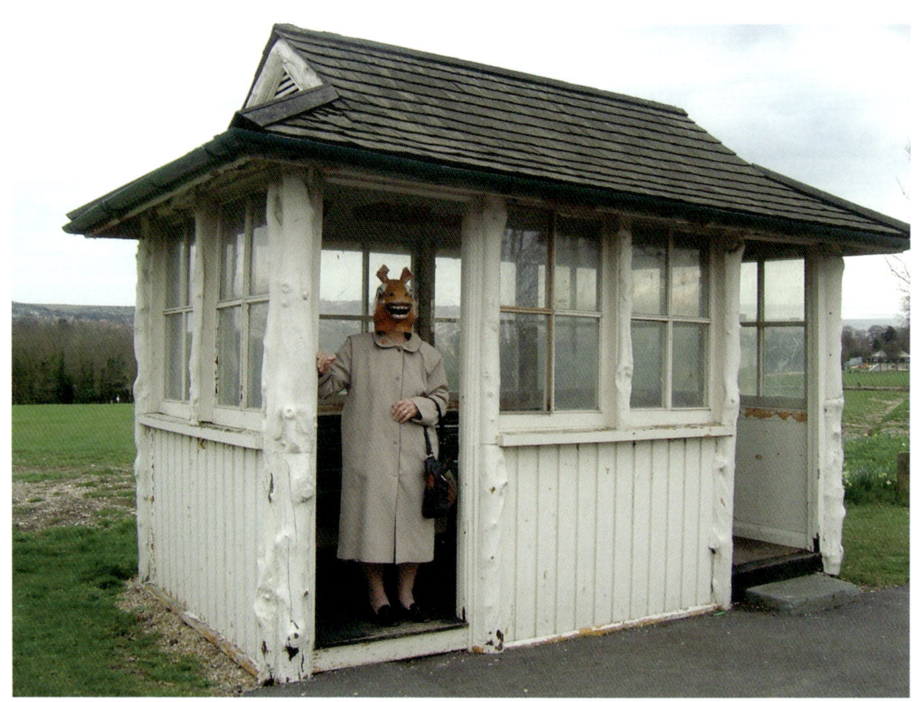

BETTY & AND THE BUS SHELTER

"For George VI's Jubilee, the Corporation decorated one tram with an illuminated Prince of Wales feather. We used to get on the trams at this shelter and I'd ask my dad if we could wait for the special tram to come around." – Eileen

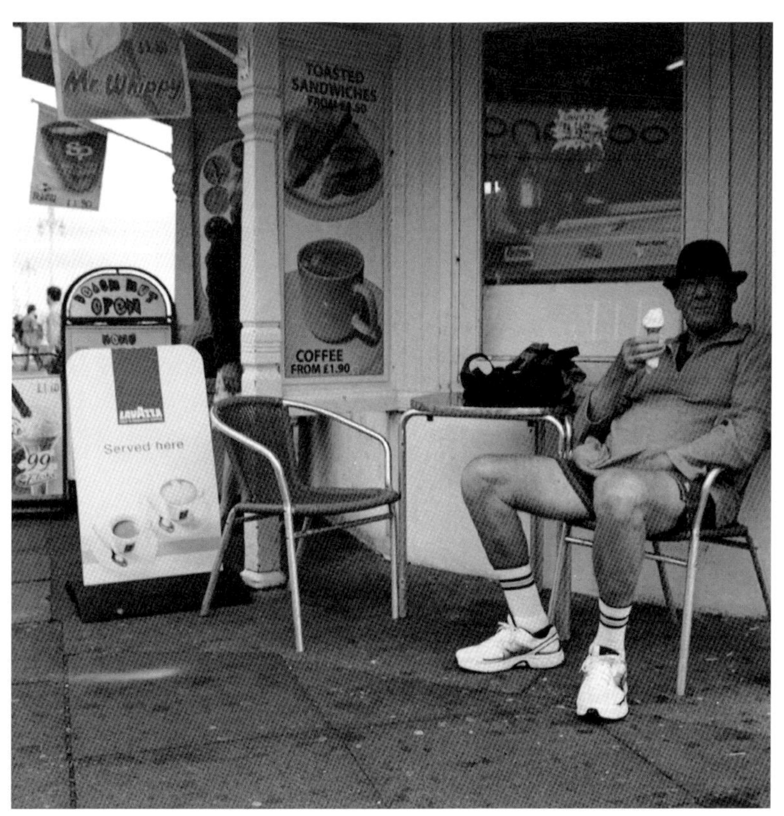

A SIT DOWN BY THE SEASIDE, AUGUST 2010

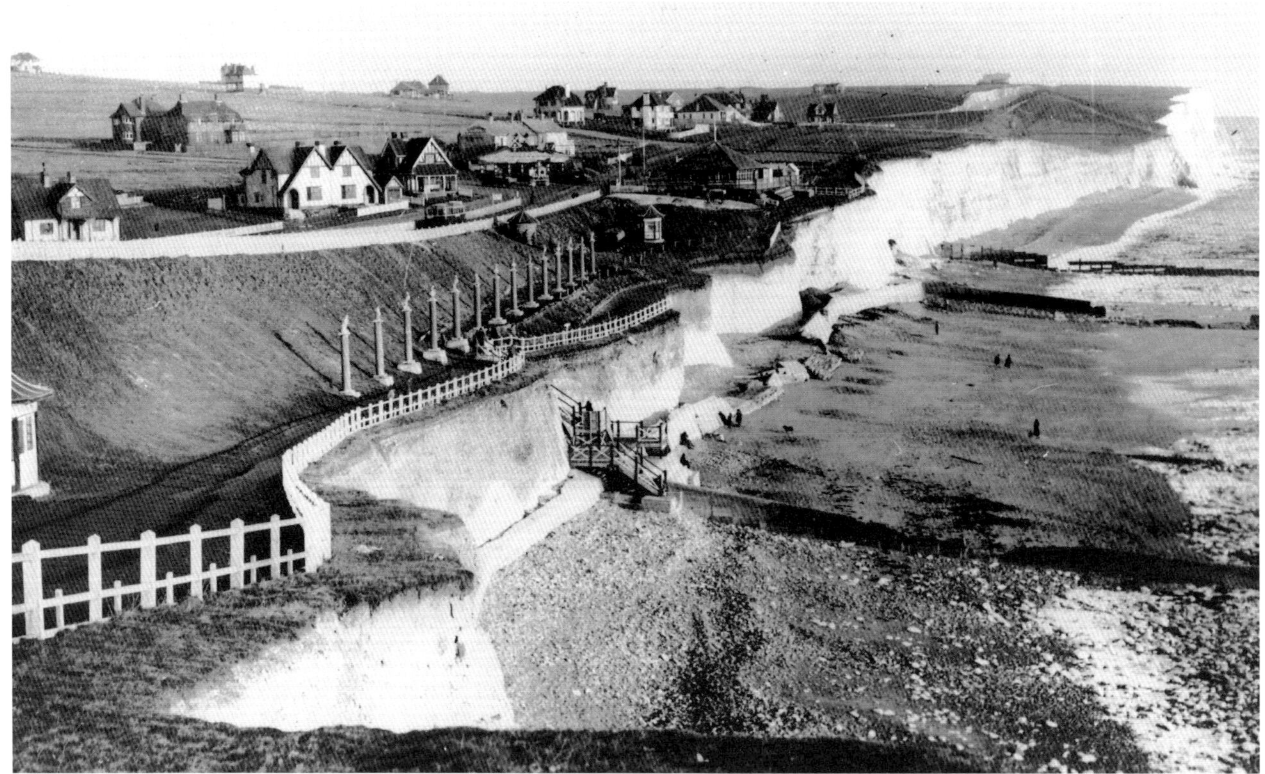

SALTDEAN IN THE 1920S

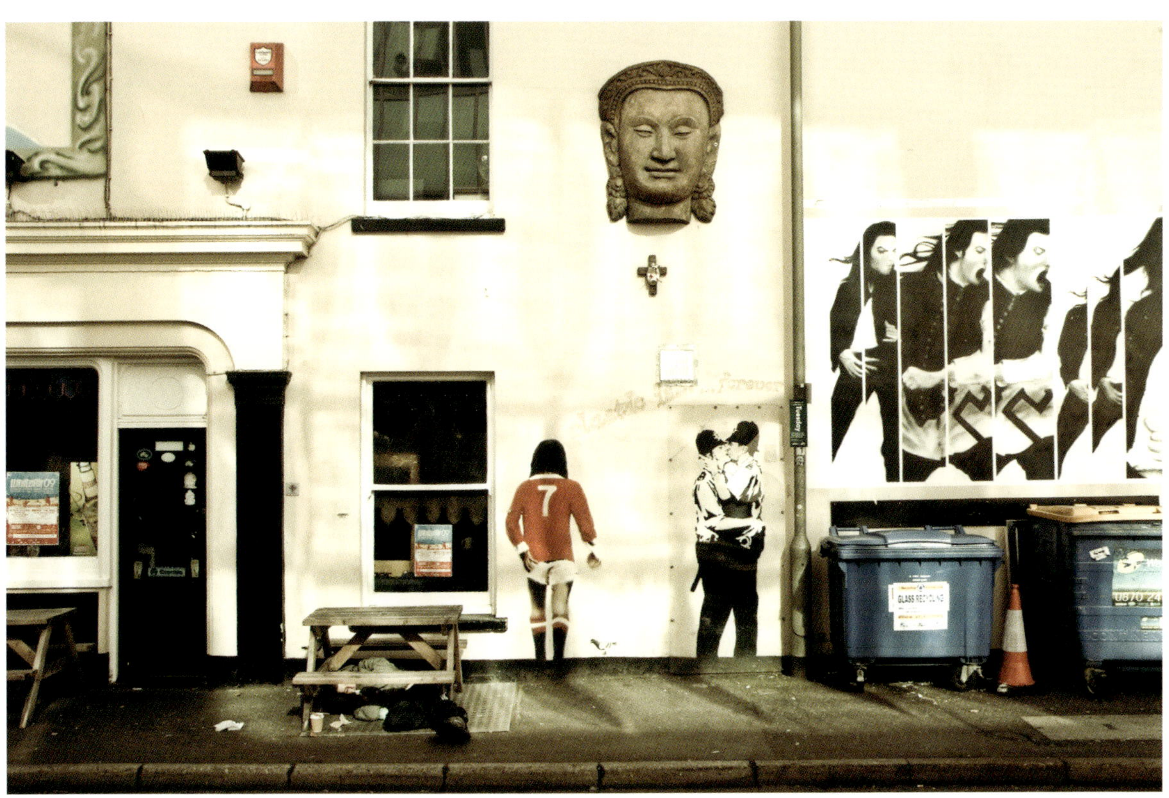

BANKSY WAS HERE

"I think they took this off the wall and sold it didn't they? Which is wrong because it is supposed to be street art, not in a gallery." – Elaine

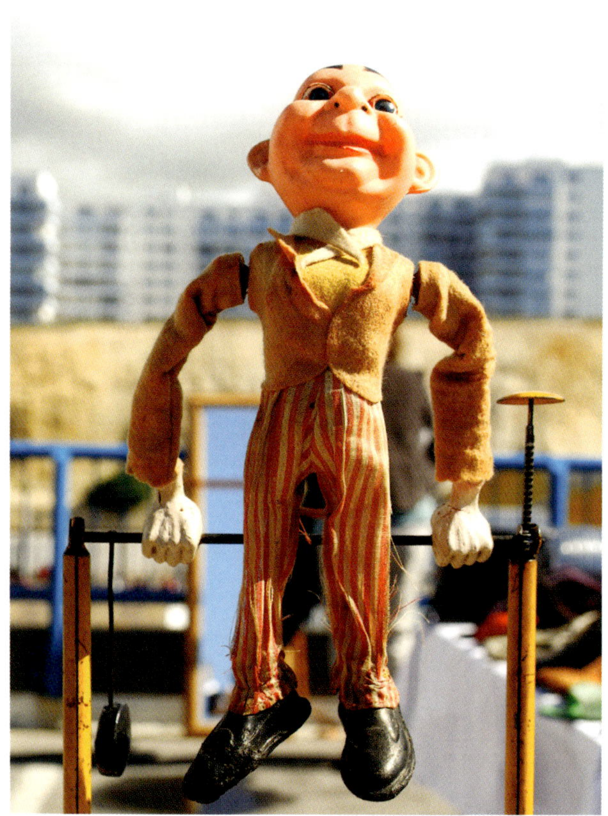

JIMMY

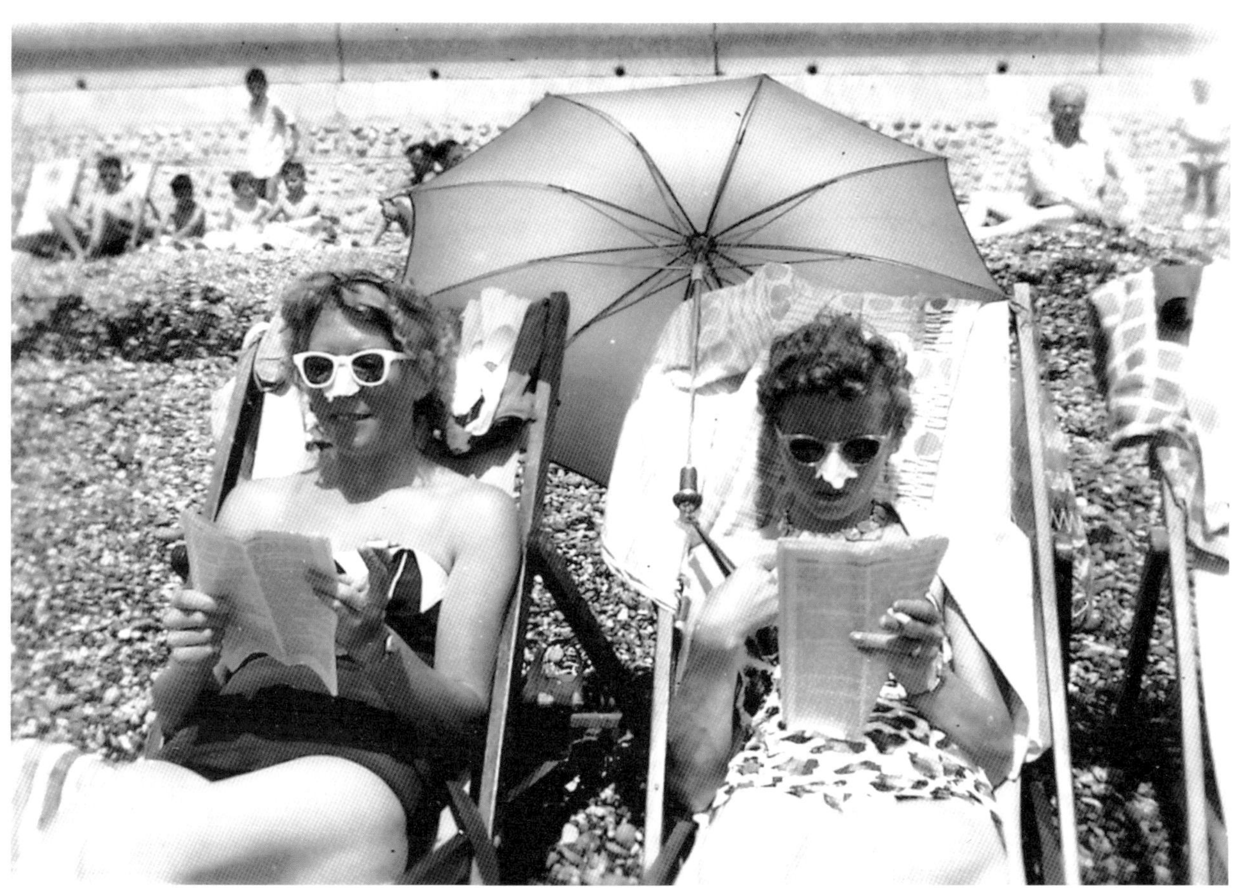

NOSECONES ON SALTDEAN BEACH

"In the 1960's people wore these on the beach because the only sun tan lotion was oil which ran down your nose. If you didn't have a cardboard cone, leaves were a good substitute!" – Laine

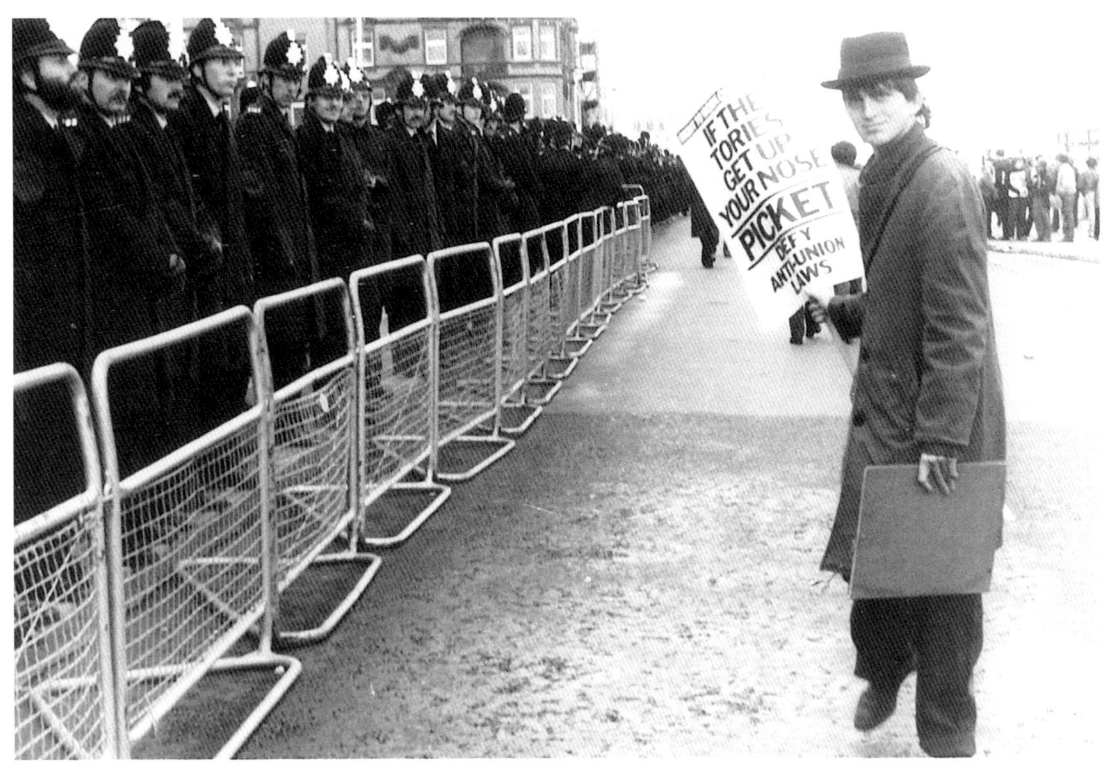

TORY CONFERENCE 10 OCTOBER 1980

©Peter Chrisp

"The History book on the shelf is always repeating itself... (Abba)." – Andrew

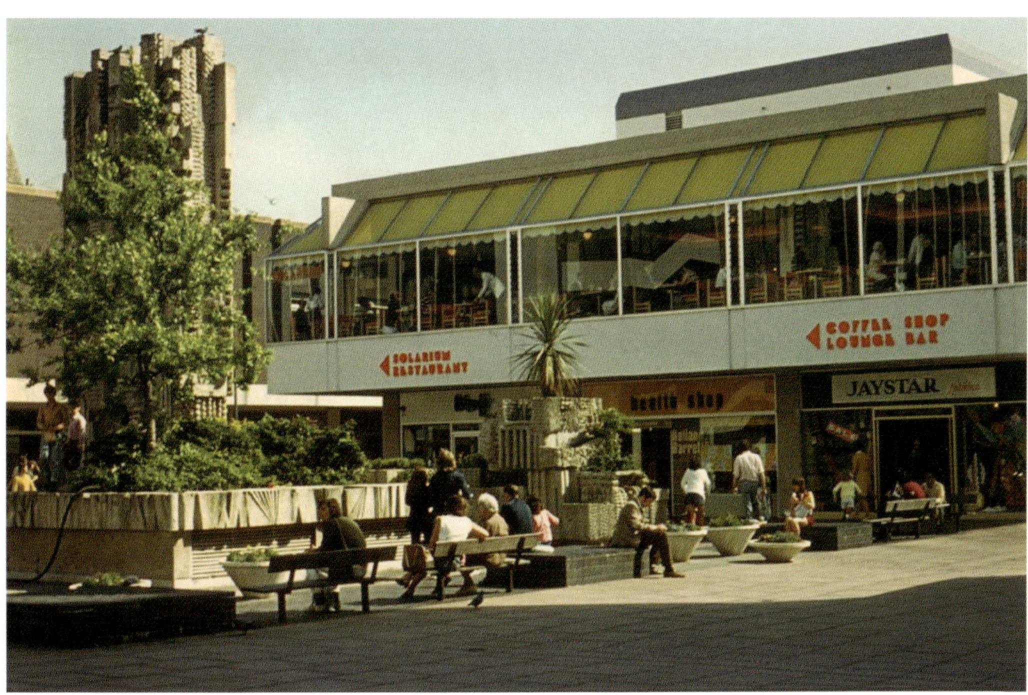

CHURCHILL SQUARE 1972

©Reinard Clasen

"My kids used to climb up the concrete plant holders" – Andrea

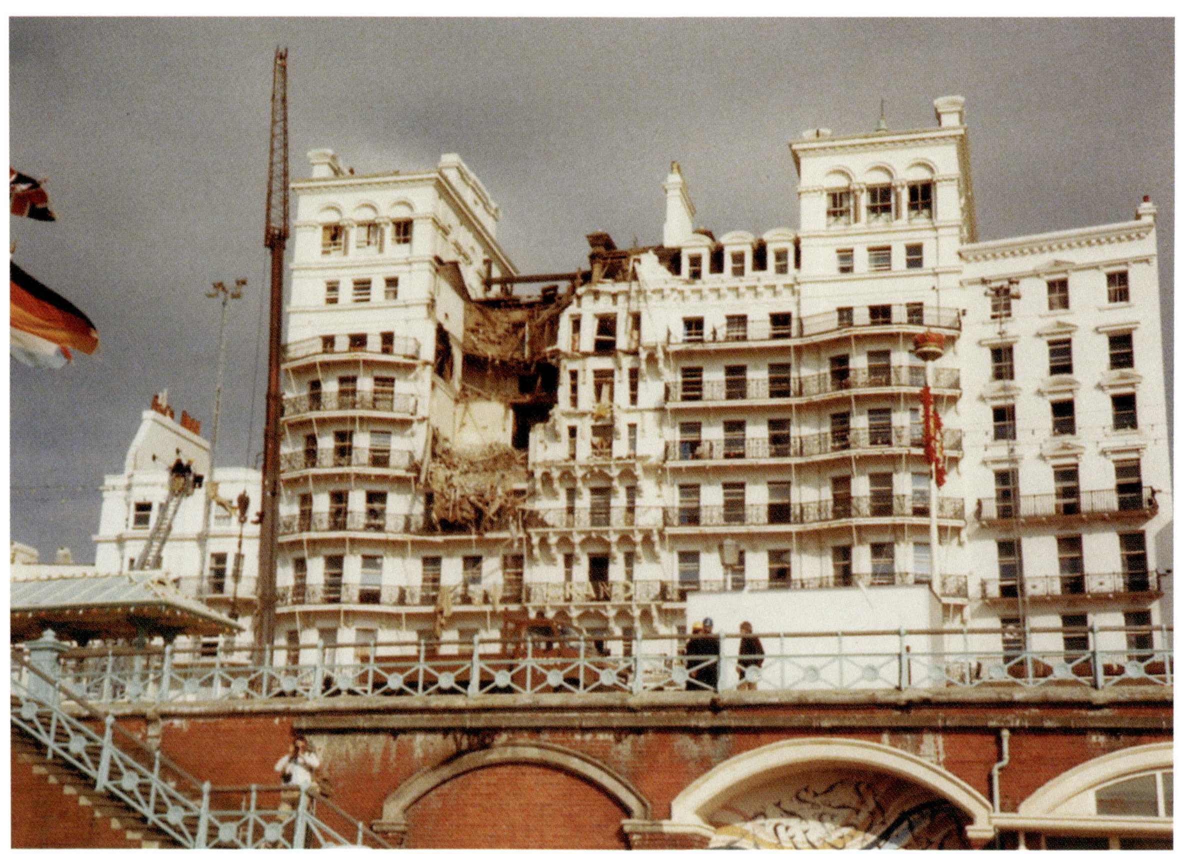

GRAND HOTEL BOMBED, 1984

"I was there. We lived around the corner and I recall the helicopter and the police. We were afraid to go out because there was such a police presence. We thought we'd be shot. It was like being in a war zone." – Richard

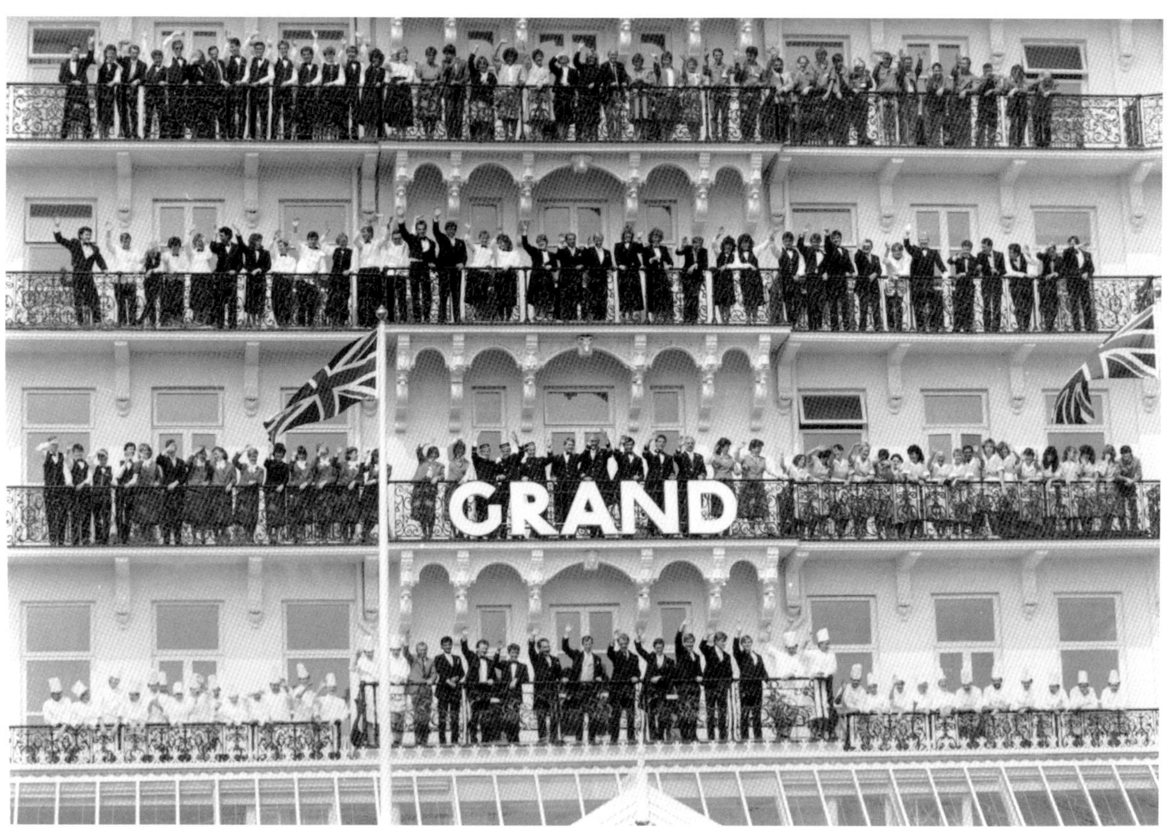

THE GRAND HOTEL RE-OPENS AFTER THE BOMB

"The manager from Marks & Spencers was there on the night it was bombed and he opened up the shop to give the Cabinet new clothes." – Gemma

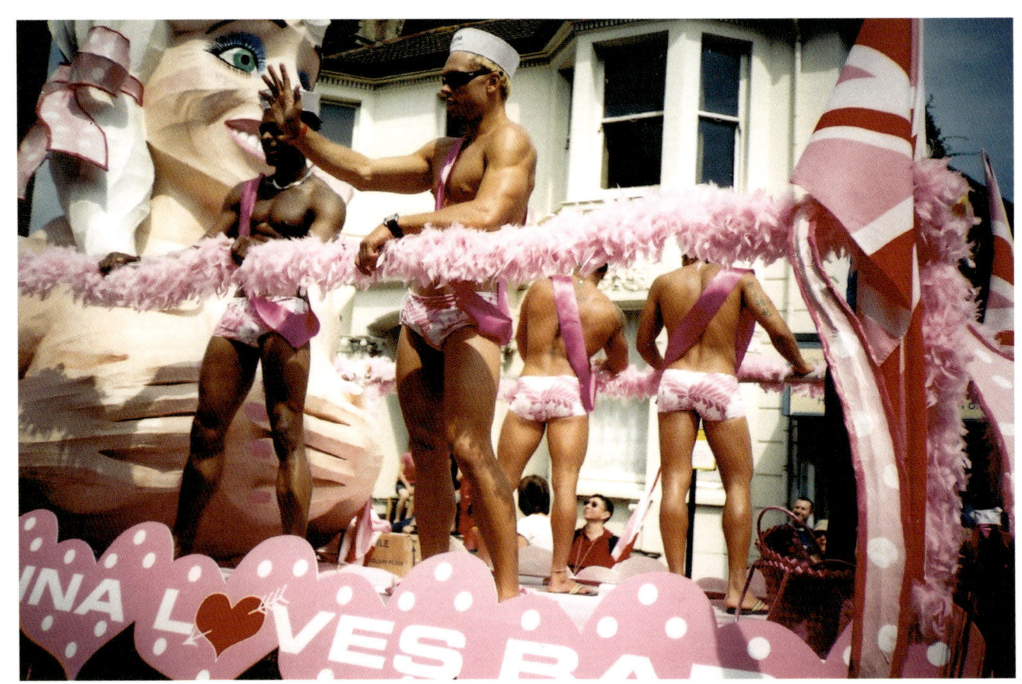

PRIDE

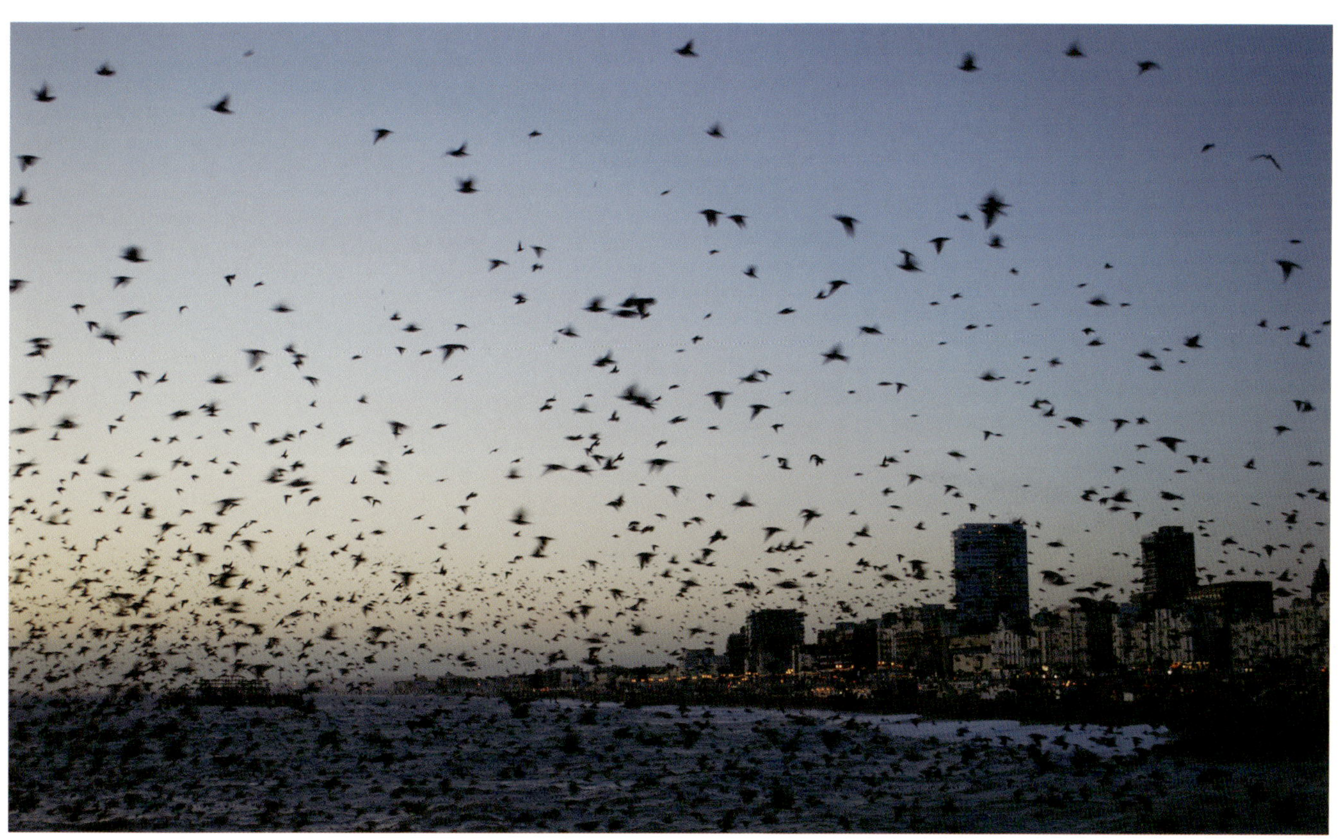

STARLINGS AT SUNSET

www.photosbrightonandhove.org.uk

Published by QueenSpark Books

QueenSpark is a non-profit-making community publishing and writing organisation which has helped the people of Brighton & Hove tell their stories since 1972.

QueenSpark Books
Room 207
University of Brighton
10-11 Pavilion Parade
Brighton BN2 1RA
Tel. 01273 571710
www.queensparkbooks.org.uk

QueenSpark would like to gratefully acknowledge the financial support given by the following individuals in order to produce this book:

Shaun Oaten
Margaretta Jolly
Virginia Nicholson
Clair Farenden
Jackie Blackwell
Jonathan Prichard
David Sewell

Book design & cover illustration: Harrison & Co | www.harrisonandco.com

ISBN: 978-0-904733-83-9

A catalogue record of this book is available from the British Library.

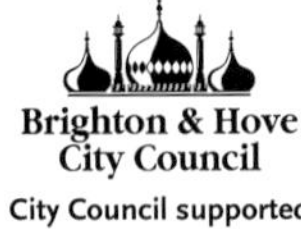

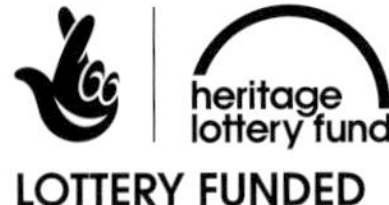